CONTENTS

FOREWORD

THE GREATEST LESSON

A Course in Miracles teaches that we have but two basic emotions. These are fear and love. All others are derivatives of these two. Further, one of the basic emotions cannot exist in the presence of the other. As John wrote: "True love casts out all fear." Jesus tried to teach the lesson of love to the world two thousand years ago and humanity is still struggling with it.

We have learned to live in fear — fear of nuclear holocaust, fear of poverty, fear of illness, fear of loneliness, fear of death. Fear distorts our vision of others, ourselves, and the world. The way we "see" is learned over time and becomes ingrained in our personality. Psychologists refer to the phenomenon of how we make sense of what we see as selective perception. Not only do we as individuals have ingrained patterns of selective perception, but families, groups and nations develop similar patterns. Sociologists state that people collectively share meanings about the world they live in through a common culture. They teach us that reality is socially constructed.

Great spiritual leaders have told us that we can choose to see differently, to live differently, to cast aside fear and become truly loving. The ancient Greeks described three types of love: eros, which is sexually based; filial or brotherly love; and agape, an unconditional love. If we choose to, we can pursue the path of brotherly and unconditional love which helps us to cast out fear and see the "reality" of the world differently. Many things, including our own perceptions and those of others, lead us into fear and off the path of love.

Genevieve Weirich has spent years developing an approach to help people who choose to pursue the path of love. This book, entitled *Attitudinal Healing, a Guide for Groups and Individuals*, is the culmination of her efforts to date. It introduces some concepts that are basic to seeing the world in a different way. Following the systematic process outlined in this book will help the reader practice the application of concepts necessary to break through and move beyond their own selective perceptions. For maximum utility this book should be used in a group. This approach provides an opportunity to learn and to discuss the results of the application of new concepts within a setting where one is accepted, encouraged and supported.

Genevieve's book will provide a useful framework for people who lead a group. It will assist the leader and the participants to question and begin to modify their previous patterns of selective perception and to help all to question the dominant thought patterns of the culture which have been enshrined through the social construction of reality.

I believe that Genevieve Weirich has developed a very useful tool to help us in our efforts to become less fearful and more loving. This is the greatest lesson we have to learn.

Jerry Wilson, PhD., has taught college for fifteen years, focusing on human behavior and the social environment, social policy, curriculum development and counseling. He has directed Community Mental Health programs for fourteen years, developing new programs for the developmentally disabled, mentally ill, alcohol and drug abusers and troubled families. He is a member of the Board of Directors of the Attitudinal Healing Center of Grand Rapids.

ACKNOWLEDGMENTS

I have learned that all the people I encounter in my life teach me and that we are all teachers and students to each other. I am grateful to all of you who have taught me a greater understanding of myself and others, and to forgive and love more often. Many of you are named in the book as writers, facilitators of groups, group members, scientists, children, family, associates, friends, teachers, students and artists. May I say thank you to all of you for loving, supporting, teaching and challenging me on this journey we call life and for your unique, individual contributions to this book.

I gratefully acknowledge The John E. Fetzer Institute of Kalamazoo, Michigan, for providing partial funding for the creation of the original copy, entitled *Attitudinal Healing Facilitator Training Manual*.

Genevieve Weirich
Grand Rapids, Michigan
September, 1991

INTRODUCTION

This book was written as a guide and resource for individuals and groups whose goal is to experience greater inner peace through the process we call "attitudinal healing". It describes my own process of growth and I hope it can be a tool for other's growth.

"Attitudinal healing" is a process of shifting the way we perceive, and can be defined as a process of releasing our fears so we can experience our natural state, which is to be loving and peaceful. As we choose to change our fearful attitudes, we are free to let go of the past and to live in the moment; to forgive ourselves and others; to feel our connectedness with others; to feel loved. The healed mind trusts that the world is governed by a power in it but not of it and that power is love — the most important healing power in the world. And that power will guide us to the extent we trust it and remember to call upon it.

The book was written as a program to train volunteers to facilitate peer support programs in Attitudinal Healing Centers for people in the social services who want to learn the attitudinal healing model of helping in their professional work and for people who wish to experience life more peacefully no matter what the circumstances. The purpose of the programs is not just to join people in crisis but to bring more joy and peace to all of us in all relationships. We believe we are all students and teachers to each other.

The Attitudinal Healing Centers are organizations through which these concepts can be experienced and learned. The first of the numerous Centers which presently exist worldwide was founded by Gerald Jampolsky, M.D., who also wrote *Love is Letting Go of Fear*. In his work in the oncology ward of a hospital, he became aware that children facing cancer were struggling emotionally and spiritually as well as physically. He realized children had no environment in which to discuss their concerns about their illnesses or their fears about death. Developing a peer support group to supplement medical treatment, Dr. Jampolsky and other volunteers found that even when children were feeling isolated, fearful and angry about their disease, they could begin to experience peace, love and meaning in their lives by reaching out and supporting another child. This approach was so successful that groups for the siblings and parents of the children were soon started.

Although the main focus of the Centers' programs continues to be support for children with serious illnesses and their families, the programs have expanded in many centers. They may include peer support for people of all ages who are experiencing feelings of separation due to serious or chronic illness, physical loss, loss of a family member or emotional distress, as well as people who want to live life more fully.

The concepts taught in this book are often expressed in Christian terminology but are ecumenical in nature, and congruent with the perennial philosophy and universal truths prevalent in all religions. Concepts from *A Course in Miracles*[1], many of which are described in *Love is Letting Go of Fear*, are used in the cognitive framework of this study.

The picture of the child on the first page was drawn by one of the children at our Center. To me, it symbolizes our goal to experience that innocent, joyful, trusting child in us—the divine.

This book is a guide and resource book to be modified and adapted to local or individual circumstances, experiences and needs. It is not static, but dynamic, intended to stimulate ideas and creativity. It is not an end but rather a means in the group process toward our own healing and the healing of others.

The ultimate goal of this book is that it be an instrument for people to find their own light and radiate that light throughout their world so as to bring greater peace to the hearts of all.

Genevieve Weirich
1145 Cambridge S.E.
Grand Rapids, MI 49506
(616) 245-0045

THE AUTHOR

Genevieve Weirich is the Director of the Attitudinal Healing Center of Grand Rapids, Michigan. She began her work with attitudinal healing in 1980 at the Family Cancer Support Network in Evanston, Illinois. Since that time she has led attitudinal healing groups and instructed several hundred people in training programs. She has assisted in developing new centers and training programs in Michigan, Alabama, New York City and the Dominican Republic, for hospital, school, church and mental health staffs, and for volunteers. She enjoys describing the meaning, joy and peace that the experiences the attitudinal healing center programs and participants have brought into her life.

Genevieve Weirich's entire life has been a school house of rich experiences, many of which illustrate the concepts described in this book. During World War II she served with the American Red Cross in Hawaii, and in Germany with the Army of Occupation. She and her husband, Paul, have raised three children. For nine years, while her children were small, she served on their school's Board of Directors. She taught Special Problems of Middle Age, and Intergenerational Communications at Northeastern Illinois University in Chicago where she obtained her Master's degree in Special Education. She was an elementary school Special Education teacher in Arlington Heights, Illinois, and studied psychology as a post Master's student at the Illinois School of Professional Psychology in Chicago for two years.

In 1989, an around-the-world voyage on the SS Universe, Semester at Sea, sponsored by the University of Pittsburgh, gave her an opportunity to meet with local health care and religious leaders in many ports: Kobe, Japan, Keelung, Taiwan, Hong Kong, Penang, Malaysia, Madras, India, Odessa, USSR, Istanbul, Turkey, Dubrovnick, Yugoslavia, Casablanca, Morocco. She reported that the people she met were searching for ways to heal symptoms of fear and separation and to find more harmonious ways to live.

The participants in her many attitudinal healing workshops, both in the United States and overseas, include people from all walks of life. They come to these workshops because they want to experience greater harmony in their personal and professional lives, or perhaps to learn to facilitate peer support groups.

NOTE TO THE READER

This book is divided into twelve sessions for presentation. However, far more program suggestions are included than can be covered in the twelve sessions. The resources in the Background Information for Trainers section can be used for programs also. It is suggested that the trainer read the entire book before planning the program content and number of sessions. It is important to plan at least thirty minutes of sharing time for each session so that participants can experience attitudinal healing in the group.

Love is Letting Go of Fear, Gerald Jampolsky, M.D., CELESTIALARTS, Berkley, CA, 1979, is a necessary auxiliary book since frequent reading assignments are made in this book.

I welcome letters about your experiences using this book. Your comments and suggestions will guide me in making changes and additions in future printings.

DEFINITION OF ATTITUDINAL HEALING

"Attitudinal healing" is the process of releasing our fears so that we can experience our natural state which is to be loving and peaceful. As we choose to change our fearful attitudes, we are free to let go of the past and to live in the moment, to forgive ourselves and others, to feel our connectedness with others, and to feel loved. The healed mind trusts that the world is governed by a power in it but not of it; that power is love, the most important healing power in the world. And that power will guide us to the extent we trust it and remember to call upon it.

ESSENTIAL CONCEPTS OF ATTITUDINAL HEALING

1.   Healing is described as inner peace and is achieved through forgiveness.

2.   We forgive ourselves and others by turning our grievances over to our Universal Mind, the Higher Power within us, God.

3.   We are free to love ourselves and others when our fears are released. Our natural state is to love.

4.   Giving love and receiving love are the same.

5.   Our minds are connected, thus love and energy may be extended to others not only in their presence, but through the miles.

6.   Life is eternal. Death is a transition to another level of existence.

7.   This moment is the only time there is since the past is over and the future is yet to be.

8.   Each of us is responsible for our thoughts. We can exchange our fear thoughts for thoughts of inner peace.

9.   We are all students and teachers to each other.

10.   All loving responses by ourselves or others extend love and all fearful responses are a call for love.

11.   The world is governed by a power that is in us but not of us. That power is love, the most important healing force.

12.   We can be guided by the power that is in us but not of us to the extent we trust it and remember to ask for it.

GOALS OF TRAINING PROGRAM

1.   Participants begin to use the essential concepts of attitudinal healing and the attitudinal healing group experience of the training program to heal the attitudes which inhibit inner peace.

2.   Participants improve their ability to listen without judging and analyzing.

3.   Participants learn the psychological aspects of loss.

4.   Participants experience the use of music, art, visualization and meditation as ways of releasing fear.

5.   Participants begin to forgive themselves and the "button pushers" in their lives.

6.   Participants examine their feelings about death in order to lessen their fear of death so as to live more fully.

7.   Participants begin to release their fears so as to experience the greatest possible love in their lives.

8.   Participants become aware of their conflicts and see their resolution during the transition to new perceptions, which brings greater inner peace.

9.   Participants learn to facilitate an attitudinal healing peer support group.

ATTITUDINAL HEALING TRAINING PROGRAM OUTLINE

Session 1   Introductions
The definition of "attitudinal healing" and the goals and format of the training program are presented. A Lesson from *Love Is Letting Go of Fear* is assigned for daily study and weekly discussion.

Session 2   Healing as Inner Peace
Important attitudinal healing concepts described in this training program are discussed.

Session 3   Getting Acquainted and Listening
Exercises designed to enhance listening skills and learning to know one another better.

Session 4   Role of Facilitator and Format of Meeting
The role of the facilitator and the format of an attitudinal healing meeting are presented.

Session 5   Psychological Aspects of Grief
The process of dealing with loss is examined.

Session 6   Using Your Imagination
Ways in which art, music, meditation and visualization can be used to express feelings.

Session 7   Forgiveness Workshop
The process of forgiveness is discussed.

Session 8   Forgiveness Workshop Continued
A process for forgiving the "button pushers" in our lives is presented and experienced.

Session 9   Fears Experienced with Serious Illness
The effects of a life-threatening condition and the fear of death on the ill person, family members, and the facilitator are discussed.

Session 10 Releasing Blocks to Love
A process of releasing the fears which prevent us from experiencing the greatest possible love in our lives.

Session 11 Transition

The conflict and the resolution of feelings that result from new perceptions about self and relationships is discussed.

Session 12 Summary

A review of attitudinal healing concepts described in this book and ways to apply them in all relationships.

Session 1

Introductions

Session 1

INTRODUCTIONS

I.   PURPOSE

1. Introduce group members.

2. Learn the format of the training meetings.

3. Discuss "meditation" and its purpose in attitudinal healing training.

4. Discuss the definition of "attitudinal healing."

5. Discuss the goals of attitudinal healing training.

II.   PROCEDURE

1. Introduction of group members

Ask each person to describe experiences which have motivated them to participate in this training program.

2. Format of training meetings

Explain that the first part of each meeting will be facilitated as an attitudinal healing group so the participants can experience the process of attitudinal healing. In the last part of the session, the trainers will focus on the subject of the evening.

The meetings will be opened with a visualization and meditation.

Dr. Gerald Jampolsky's book, *Love Is Letting Go of Fear*, is used as a text for the training. A lesson from that text will be assigned each week. The lesson will be written on a card at each meeting so that it is available to be read frequently each day. Key paragraphs from the assigned lesson and chapter will be read at the following meeting. Members will have an opportunity to share a personal experience which has helped them understand the concept, or an experience which would have been less fearful if they had remembered the concept.

3. **Group process in attitudinal healing**

(In an attitudinal healing group of seriously ill children, for example, after the meditation and visualization, we could ask but would not insist, that each child in the circle introduce himself and describe a fearful experience and a happy event in his life since the last meeting.)

A member in the training group, as in any other attitudinal healing group, who wants to share intense feelings, such as grief, anger, anxiety, sadness, or panic, should be allowed full expression of his or her experiences and feelings. The other members have an opportunity to help by listening or relating how they have experienced the same feelings and how they dealt with them. We learn from this sharing of feelings and experience that as we help another person we help ourselves. For example, in a children's group, when seven year old Eric explained to a new member what he could expect when he got his first brain scan, he said, "I forgot I was sick when I told him about my brain scan so he wouldn't be scared. I feel good inside when I help someone."

It is important that the members feel accepted, safe and understood so they are free to express their fears and joys. The training is a place to practice listening without judgment and to practice accepting one another. The experience of being listened to and of feeling accepted teaches us even more about attitudinal healing than does the intellectual understanding of the concepts.

Remind the group about the importance of confidentiality in the group.

4. **Meditation and visualization**

Teach the "balloon" visualization in the following paragraph which was created by the children at the Tiburon, California Center. Children like to do this imagery over and over just as they enjoy reading a familiar book many times. Adults enjoy the simplicity of this visualization and like it almost as much as children.

"Close your eyes and take three deep breaths to quiet your mind. Visualize a large garbage can with the lid lying beside it. A large yellow helium filled balloon is attached to the lid. Allow your fears and attack thoughts to come into your minds and observe yourself as in a movie putting these thoughts into the garbage can. Put the lid on the can and watch the balloon lift the can with all the fears into the sky, higher and higher, until the can and all the fears it contains are out of sight."

One facilitator told us about a visualization she imaged just before she visited a patient in the hospital or started facilitating a group. She visualized corks in each of her toes. She released all her frustrations, anxieties and fears from the top of her head to her toes. She pulled the corks out of her toes and all those fears drained out and looked like yellow "gucky" stuff. She hung her "ego" on a hook outside the door before entering the room where her group met or a hospital room, and she was free to listen, accept and love.

5. Purpose of "meditation" in attitudinal healing

Discuss meditation as described in this session.

6. Definition of "attitudinal healing"

Read and discuss the definition found on page 8

7. Goals of attitudinal healing

Discuss the goals as outlined on page 10

8. Lesson

Read lesson 1, "All That I Give I Give to Myself," page 49, in *Love Is Letting Go of Fear*, and discuss its meaning.

9. Assignments

Give the members copies of the "Prayer for Guidance," from *A Course in Miracles, Text* included in this session and suggest they memorize it to be used as a prayer before facilitating attitudinal healing groups, and in their personal lives.

Assign lesson 2, page 63, in *Love Is Letting Go of Fear*, "Forgiveness Is the Key to Happiness," for the following week. Stress the importance of daily study. Give the members cards and ask them to write the lesson sentence at the meeting so it can be carried with them all week.

Assign Dr. Jampolsky's books, *Teach Only Love* and *Good-bye to Guilt*, for home reading during the twelve week training.

Assign "Self-Esteem" supplement in "Resources" at end of book.

10. Closing

Close the meeting by holding hands, standing in a circle with a short statement of gratitude or a song. A statement such as "I am happy I could meet all of you tonight and I look forward to seeing you next week" is appropriate.

III.   BACKGROUND INFORMATION FOR TRAINERS

1. "Love One Another" (included in this session)

2. *Love Is Letting Go of Fear* concepts (included in this session)

3. "Jeremy" (Resource section)

4. "The Gospel as Yoga" (Resource section)

IV.   SUGGESTED READING

1. Dass, Ram. *Journey of Awakening.*

2. Jampolsky, Gerald G., M.D. *Good-Bye to Guilt.*

3. Jampolsky, Gerald G., M.D. *Teach Only Love.*

4. Jampolsky, Gerald G., M.D. *To Give is to Receive - An 18 Day Course in Healing Relationships and Bringing About Peace of Mind.*

MEDITATION

"Meditation" in our training can be described as a quiet time or a prayerful time. Its purpose is to relax our body and mind and to allow the thoughts from our busy day to come into our awareness so that we can release them and feel more centered. When we quiet ourselves in a group we can feel joined with the other members. This joining or feeling of unity dissipates our feelings of separateness and loneliness.

Each training session opens with a meditation and visualization. After we quiet ourselves through counting our breathing, taking several deep breaths or doing a body relaxation exercise we often visualize ourselves in a place where we can release our thoughts, as to the clouds, water, fire or waves, so we can feel more peaceful. When our minds are joined to release our thoughts, we feel a strength in that union and that strength is love, the power that heals our attitudes.

Many people who meditate daily report they are freer of stress, their concentration improves, their self awareness increases and their physical energy improves. Classes are available which teach a variety of ways to learn to meditate. If you wish to participate in a more formal training, you must choose for your self which method is most effective for you.

Below I have described one method which has been helpful to me.

Begin in a sitting position with your eyes closed and concentrate on your breathing. Count each breath from one to five and then repeat counting breaths from one to five until you feel centered. If your body feels tense, relax it by imagining that your inhaled breath reaches first into your toes, then your ankles, the calves of your legs, knees, thighs, lower torso, stomach, heart, lungs, fingers, arms, throat, tongue, nose, eyes, brain, the top of your head, until you feel relaxed. As thoughts come to mind, do not try to push them down. Let them come and picture them as pink clouds or as leaves falling into a fast flowing river. Do not judge the thoughts as good or bad; judge them all equally as just thoughts.

The first week, meditate twice daily, in the morning and evening, for five minutes. Increase the time weekly to 10, 15 and then 20 minutes twice daily.

Ram Dass' book, *Journey of Awakening, A Meditator's Guidebook*, is a good resource book on meditation.

LOVE ONE ANOTHER

Since love is the greatest healing force, the teaching to "love one another" describes the basic principle of the process of healing and inner peace. That teaching is ecumenical in nature; a universal truth taught in all religions. Scriptures which express that truth are quoted here.

> What is hateful to you, do not to your fellowmen. That is the entire Law; all the rest is commentary. (*Talmud*, Shabbat, 31a.)

> He who hates no creature and is friendly and compassionate to all, who is free from attachment and egotism, equal-minded in pleasure and pain, and forgiving; who is ever content and meditative, self- subjugated and possessed with firm conviction, with mind and intellect dedicated to Me, he who is thus devoted to Me is dear to Me. (*Paramananda* p. 126)
> —Teachings of Krishna

You must so adjust your heart that you long for the welfare of all beings, including the happiness of your enemies. If a man foolishly does me wrong, I will return to him the protection of my ungrudging love; the more evil comes from him, the more good shall go from me ... Let us live happily then, not hating those who hate us. Among men who hate us let us dwell free from hatred ... With pure thoughts and fullness of love, I will do towards others what I would do for myself. (*Paramananda* p. 127)
    —Buddha

To the good I would be good. To the not- good I would also be good in order to make them good. Recompense injury with kindness ... Of all noble qualities, loving compassion is the noblest. (*Paramananda* p. 128)
    —Laotze

Love your enemies, bless them that curse you, do good to them that hate you, and pray for them that despitefully use you, and persecute you; that ye may be the children of your Father which is in Heaven ... Do unto others what ye would have others do unto you. (*Matt. 5:44, Luke 6:31*)
    —Jesus Christ

You will not enter paradise until you have faith; and you will not complete your faith till you love one another. (*Syed* p. 40)
    —Prophet Muhammad

LOVE IS LETTING GO OF FEAR CONCEPTS

1. All that I Give is Given to Myself. (p. 51)

2. Forgiveness is the Key to Happiness. (p. 65)

3. I Am Never Upset for the Reason I Think. (p. 71)

4. I Am Determined to See Things Differently. (p. 77)

5. I Can Escape from the World I See by Giving Up Attack Thoughts. (p. 85)

6. I Am Not a Victim of the World I See. (p. 91)

7. Today I Will Judge Nothing that Occurs. (p. 97)

8. This Instant is the Only Time There Is. (p. 105)

9. The Past is Over, It Can Touch Me Not. (p. 111)

10. I Could See Peace Instead of This. (p. 117)

11. I Can Elect to Change All Thoughts that Hurt. (p. 123)

12. I Am Responsible for What I See. (p. 129)

From: Jampolsky, Gerald, M.D. *Love Is Letting Go of Fear*, published by Celestial Arts, Berkeley, CA.

Prayer for Guidance

*I am here only to be
truly helpful.
I am here to represent
him who sent me.
I do not have to worry
about what to say
or what to do,
because he who sent me
will direct me.
I am content to be
wherever he wishes,
knowing he goes there
with me.
I will be healed
as I let him
teach me to heal.*

Session 2

Healing as Inner Peace

Session 2

HEALING AS INNER PEACE

I.   PURPOSE

1. Introduce concepts of attitudinal healing.

2. Discuss the attitudinal healing concept, "Forgiveness is the Key to Happiness", lesson 2 in *Love Is Letting Go of Fear*.

3. Discuss the meaning of "inner peace".

4. Learn the philosophy of attitudinal healing by viewing TV video "Donahue and Kids" if it is available.

II.   PROCEDURE

1. Visualization and meditation

Ask the group members to close their eyes and quiet their minds by taking several deep breaths. Guide them through the following imagery.

Visualize a small light at the heart center of each person and watch that light grow to cover the entire body of each person until there is a circle of light. That light is love, the greatest healing force in the world. Put into that circle of light all those people you wish to forgive or to bless. (Time) Now join all minds as One without limit to send love to people who need it. (Time) Return your thoughts to the room.

It is helpful to end all adult meditations with the joining of minds *without limit* to channel love to the world. This is an opportunity to experience the concept, "To give love is to receive love." End with the "Prayer for Guidance."

2. Lesson

Read key paragraphs from lesson 2, page 65, "Forgiveness is the Key to Happiness," in *Love Is Letting Go of Fear*. If the group is larger than fourteen people, divide the group into two groups. Invite each member to relate an experience in which this lesson helped them to see something more peacefully or when it might have helped them if they had remembered it.

3. Healing as inner peace

Suggest that the members describe an experience in which they felt inner peace.

In attitudinal healing, we describe healing as inner peace. All of us have experienced inner peace if only for a fleeting instant or a short period of time. Our desire is to lengthen that time of peace in our daily lives.

The participants will probably use some of the following phrases when they describe how they felt during this peaceful time. Recap some of their descriptions and add the concepts listed below.

We feel one with nature.
We are often alone, but not lonesome.
We feel safe, protected.
We experience the moment as if there is no past or future, no time.
We do not judge ourselves or others.
We do not analyze the situation.
We feel loving and loved. We experience no lack in ourselves or the experience.
All our needs are met.
We are not afraid; we have transcended our fears.
We hold no grievances.

4. Concepts of attitudinal healing

Introduce the concepts described in "Discussion of Essential Concepts of Attitudinal Healing" included in this session. Give each person a copy of the concepts.

It is not expected that all the concepts presented here will be integrated during the training. The concepts are introduced for people's consideration at the appropriate time for their growth. Attitudinal healing is an experience and the words which can guide and explain the experience need to be expressed in many ways and at the appropriate time to be relevant. The facilitator trainer can follow their intuition as to how to express the concepts and when to introduce them.

5. "Donahue and Kids"

View and discuss the TV film "Donahue and Kids" if it is available.

6. **Assignments**

Assign lesson 3, "I Am Never Upset for the Reason I Think," in *Love Is Letting Go of Fear*, page 71. Have cards available so each person can write the lesson for daily study.

Ask the members to think of the three experiences in their lives which have been the most significant in helping them understand themselves and others. Ask them to choose one to describe to the group the following week and explain how it has taught them.

7. **Closing**

Close the meeting by standing and holding hands in a circle with a statement such as, "We are grateful for the love and support we have given to one another tonight".

III.   BACKGROUND INFORMATION FOR TRAINER

The "Donahue and Kids" video may be purchased from Multimedia, 140 West Ninth Street, Cincinnati, Ohio, 45202 Telephone: (513) 352-5088.

ESSENTIAL CONCEPTS OF ATTITUDINAL HEALING

1.   Healing is described as inner peace and is achieved through forgiveness.

This statement describes a long process of change and growth. When we speak of healing, we refer to healing the attitude so that our higher self or spiritual self can manifest. The attitude is a mind set which has become a neural structure of the brain because of social conditioning. The mindset is a combination of feelings, thoughts, ideas and memories that affect perception. In order to release our negative fearful attitudes, we need to reassess our old patterns of perception and retrain our minds to respond with positive and loving attitudes. We have two emotions, love and fear. Our fears are an accumulation of experiences from the past which need to be labeled and released — forgiven. When we release the past, forgive, we are free to be our essential loving and lovable selves and experience inner peace.

2.   We forgive ourselves and others by turning our grievances over to the Universal Mind, our Higher Self, God.

We are born into the world as innocent, trusting beings. As we live we develop an ego self to protect ourself from the physical and emotional dangers we perceive in the world. In building this protective ego self we begin to feel separated from our Source and from each other. Because of our loneliness and fear we sometimes devise ruthless and manipulative ways to feel joined with others and to protect ourselves. This causes us to feel guilty.

We must desire to let go of our past and to forgive ourselves in order to find greater joy and peace. We can then transcend the ego self (the self we made) to the higher self, by turning our grievances over to the Universal Mind, God. The ego self cannot forgive the self it has made. We must turn our grievances over to the Universal Mind through the higher self — that self we experienced as innocent, trusting children.

3.   We are free to love ourselves and others when our fears are released. Our natural state is to love.

When our fears are released, we become aware of our eternally perfect self, and we are free to love.

4.   Giving love and receiving love are the same.

The laws of the world teach that to give means to have less. The Universal laws or God's laws teach that to give love to another person is to give love to ourself.

For example, in our facilitated self-help groups at the Center, we have learned that when we give love by listening without judgment to another person, we are receiving love. We are free of fears when we are listening to another person because we cannot think of ourselves when we are concentrating on another person. Love is unlimited in the Universe. It is the glue of the Universe. If we can visualize energy — love from the Universe — flowing into our minds to our hearts and then out of our hearts to love another person, we can understand visually the dynamics of the concept, "To give love is to receive love".

5.   Our minds are connected, thus love and energy may be extended to others, not only in their presence, but through the miles. As we create our ego self, we feel separated from others. When we join with one another lovingly, we have a feeling of oneness because each of us experiences the One Mind.

An image that I saw in meditation helped me understand the concept that our perfect, divine selves are connected in the One Mind where love can be extended to others.

In the image, I saw a globe of Earth. All the continents moved together and the dividing lines disappeared so that the land masses looked like one large pink cell — an amoeba. The pink represented love. The heads of all the people in the world appeared on the large amoeba. Then angel wings appeared on each individual to symbolize that we are perfect creations. The pink cell represented our One Mind where love in prayer or meditation can be extended to another person miles away.

6.   Life is eternal. Death is a transition to another level of existence.

Just as birth is a transition from eternal life to grow and learn on Earth, death is a transition for growth in another level of our eternal life. When we fear death, that fear blocks our ability to find joy in the moment and to love fully.

7.   The moment is the only time there is since the past is over and the future is yet to be.

We know the past is gone, but it cannot be gone in our minds until we release our grievances and forgive ourselves and others. When we forgive, all that is left of the past is the love we have given and received. When we release our fears of the past, we are also releasing our fears of the future and we are free to live in the moment.

8.   Each of us is responsible for our thoughts. We can exchange our fear for thoughts of peace.

A belief that thoughts and experiences in life are controlled by others, we blame others for our feelings and experiences and allow life to be limited.

When we learn that we are responsible for our thoughts and that we can choose how we react to experiences, our life becomes freer. When we know we are in control of the way we respond, we learn that with practice, we can choose peace rather than fear.

9.   We are all students and teachers of each other.

Each person we meet becomes our teacher. Each encounter gives us an opportunity to extend love or receive love, an opportunity to practice acceptance. The facilitators function as equals in the groups. Everyone teaches and all of us are equal.

10.   All loving responses by ourselves or others extend love and all fearful responses are a call for love.

When fearful responses are perceived as a call for love, we can cease to feel attacked and are free to extend love. Since our automatic response is to defend ourselves or to judge, we need to practice this new way of perceiving and call on our higher selves to help us.

11.   The world is governed by a power that is in us but not of us. That power is love, the most important healing force.

12.   We can be guided by the power that is in us but not of us to the extent we trust it and remember to ask for it.

As we dare to trust, our positive experiences teach us that trusting is trustworthy.

Session 3

Getting Acquainted
and
Listening

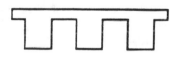

GETTING ACQUAINTED AND LISTENING

I.   PURPOSE

1. Discuss the attitudinal healing concept, "I Am Never Upset for the Reason I Think."

2. Learn the concept of "empathy" in attitudinal healing.

3. Practice non-judgmental listening.

4. Learn to know and understand one another better.

II.   PROCEDURE

1. Meditation and visualization

Ask the group members to close their eyes and quiet their minds by taking three deep breaths. Guide them through the following visualization:

Visualize yourself on a wide white sandy beach at the ocean on a cool fall evening just as the sun is setting and the moon is rising. Sea gulls soar overhead. They appear to be welcoming us by a show as they move back and forth over our heads. After they circle, they fly home to a huge rock just a few feet from the beach where we are sitting. The whole scene is to be a special gift to us. We see the bright crimson reflection of the sun on the ocean as it sets in the west, and the white, sparkling silver reflection from the moon as it rises in the southwest.
Now imagine a fire in the middle of our circle. Take time to enjoy the beauty, the feeling of oneness with each other and the earth, and feel gratitude to the earth for its gifts to us.

Let each of us think of the fears—the attack thoughts, the unforgiveness, and the guilt we want to release. Throw them into the fire, the symbol of God's power.

After a time, ask that all minds be joined as One without limit to send love to all the people in the world who need our love.

It is helpful to end with this suggestion. The power of love without limit when several people join is a great healing power. We heal our own minds when we send love and remember again that "giving love is receiving love." End with the "Prayer for Guidance."

2. Lesson

Read lesson 3, "I Am Never Upset for the Reason I Think," and ask each member to tell about a personal experience which relates to that concept. Encourage group members to listen without judgment and to relate a similar experience which might help the sharing person to feel understood. This is a time to help one another feel forgiven, accepted and loved unconditionally, a time to heal the attitudes of the group members. If the group is large, divide it into small groups.

3. Empathy

Using words which are appropriate and understandable to the group members, explain empathy as described in "True Empathy" included in this session.

4. Getting acquainted

Ask the participants to describe an experience in their lives which has taught them greater understanding of themselves and others. This exercise can teach us how all events and experiences have a purpose, often a purpose we do not understand at the time. Our most painful experiences can be the most helpful in teaching us to love and give our life meaning.

5. Listening exercise

Divide the group into pairs. The first page of the exercise (page 34) explains the process. Demonstrate the exercise using the first open-ended statement, "When I think about the future, I see myself . . .". Ask the group members to return as a group fifteen minutes before the end of the session to discuss how they experienced the exercise.

6. Assignments

Assign lesson 4, "I Am Determined to See Things Differently," page 77, *Love Is Letting Go of Fear*. Stress the importance of reading and rereading the concept each day. Ask each participant to write the concept on a card at the meeting. Suggest that the members read *Listening* by Lee Coit.

7. Closing

Close the meeting in a circle by saying, "We are thankful for this time together to support and love one another."

III.   BACKGROUND INFORMATION FOR TRAINER

Coit, Lee. *Listening*, Swan Publishing, P.O. Box 296, South Laguna, CA 92677, 1985.

TRUE EMPATHY

Empathy can be felt on the ego level or the spirit level. Empathy is connecting with the feelings of another person so that we sense the person's feeling as our own. For example, on the ego level it is helpful to feel another person's hurt, free of judgment and with total acceptance.

True empathy is a way of perceiving the other person beyond the ego, transcending the ego hurt and joining with the eternal strength of the person. When we are able to transcend and join our minds with another person's strength, that person transcends with us because our minds are connected and One. True empathy heals our minds and therefore brings peace to both of us.

We need to always ask the Holy Spirit to guide us because that is his Function. We cannot know or judge the total situation, so we must leave the judgment of what to say and do to God who will guide us perfectly. When our ego makes decisions, they are made on past perceptions which are over and cannot be used for judgment.

We must not confuse our role with God's. Let him offer us his strength and his perception to be shared through us. We are antennas for his energy and his voice. We need only ask him to enter our relationships and bless them and then not interfere.

LISTENING EXERCISE

READ SILENTLY.

A theme that is frequently voiced when people are brought together for the first time is, "I'd like to get to know you."

To get to know another person we need to learn to listen without judgment and to be willing to talk honestly about ourselves. In an understanding, nonevaluative atmosphere people are free to talk honestly about themselves to others, who then reciprocate by disclosing more about themselves.

Listening without judgment results in a greater feeling of trust, understanding, connectedness and acceptance. Relationships then become closer, allowing more significant self- disclosure and greater risk-taking. As we continue to share our experiences authentically we come to know, to trust, and to love one another.

This dyadic encounter experience is designed to facilitate getting to know another person on a fairly intimate level. The discussion items are open-ended statements and can be completed at whatever level of self-disclosure one wishes.

ALL OF THE DISCUSSION SHOULD BE KEPT CONFIDENTIAL.

Each partner responds to each statement before continuing. The statements are to be completed in the order in which they appear.

The first speaker is to complete the following item in two or three sentences.

WHEN I THINK ABOUT THE FUTURE, I SEE MYSELF.....

The partner in the exercise repeats in their own words what the first speaker has just said. The first speaker must be satisfied that they have been heard accurately.

The other partner takes their turn and completes the statement in two or three sentences. The first speaker paraphrases what the second speaker just said to the satisfaction of the second speaker.

COMPLETE THE FOLLOWING STATEMENTS IN THE SAME MANNER:

MY FAVORITE THING TO DO ON A FREE DAY IS .....

THE TIME OF THE YEAR I ENJOY THE MOST IS .....

IF I COULD PLAN A TRIP I WOULD GO TO ..... WITH ..... AND I WOULD TAKE .....

IN AMBIGUOUS, UNSTRUCTURED SITUATIONS, I .....

WHEN I AM REJECTED I USUALLY .....

I FEEL MOST AFFECTIONATE WHEN .....

WHEN I AM ALONE I USUALLY .....

I AM REBELLIOUS WHEN .....

THE EMOTION I FIND MOST DIFFICULT TO CONTROL IS .....

MY MOST FREQUENT DAYDREAMS ARE ABOUT .....

I BELIEVE IN .....

IF I COULD HAVE THREE WISHES THEY WOULD BE .....

Express how you are feeling toward your partner without using words. You may want to touch. Afterwards, tell what you intended to communicate. Also, explore how this entire communication felt.

Session 4

Role of the Facilitator
and
Format of Meeting

Session 4

ROLE OF FACILITATOR AND FORMAT OF MEETING

I.   PURPOSE

1. Learn the attitudinal healing concept, "I Am Determined to See Things Differently."

2. Learn the role of the facilitator in an attitudinal healing group.

3. Discuss the group guidelines for adults and children.

4. Discuss our personal feelings about death.

5. Learn the attitudes which teach us to truly help one another.

II.   PROCEDURE

1. Visualization and meditation

Ask the group members to close their eyes and take three deep breaths to quiet their minds for the following guided visualization and meditation:

Visualize a very tall, steep mountain topped by a beautiful, flat plateau overlooking a magnificent view of a valley and the ocean. The only way to get to the top is to take an elevator. Imagine an elevator you would like to ride in. It can be constructed in any manner, any size, and with any furnishings you want. You may choose a person or several people to go with you if you like. (Pause for a brief period of time.)

As you slowly rise in the elevator to the top of the mountain, you can view the valley below, and can stop here and there as you like. When you reach the top take time to enjoy the wondrous view. Visualize the most beautiful view you can imagine. As you look around you see that all of your group and their friends are with you. Sit in a circle on the plateau and a fire appears in the middle of the circle to warm the chilled air. You sit quietly for a while and enjoy looking into the fire. (Time) Think now of those angry thoughts and the unforgiveness which are causing you unhappiness and throw them into the fire, a symbol of the power of God who takes away all fears and forgives all. (Time)

Now join your minds as One with the Christ Mind without limit so that love can be sent wherever it is needed in the world. (Time) (The words "Christ Mind" describes the light in all religious paths.)

End with the "Prayer for Guidance."

Suggest that they open their eyes and bring their attention back to the group when they are ready.

2. Lesson

Read lesson 4, "I Am Determined to See Things Differently," page 77, from *Love Is Letting Go of Fear*, and ask each member to relate a personal experience which helped them learn the concept.

3. Format of meeting and role of facilitators

Read and discuss the "Format of Meeting and Role of Facilitator," included in this session and give a copy to each participant.

4. Death as life and growth

Read "Death as Life and Growth" and "My Teacher, Sue," included in this session, and discuss personal feelings about death.

5. How Can I Help?

Discuss the attitudes important for us to truly help another person, as described in the summary of *How Can I Help?*, Ram Dass and Paul Gorman, included in this session.

6. Group guidelines

Read and discuss the group guidelines for children and adults included with this session. The group guidelines can be read periodically at the beginning of peer support groups and the training groups.

7. Assignments

Assign lesson 5, page 85, *Love Is Letting Go of Fear*, "I Can Escape the World I See by Giving Up Attack Thoughts." Remind your members of the importance of carrying the concept in their pocket every day so they can read it over and over. Often they will find it is just the quote they need to carry them through a difficult situation at work or at home. It seems the Universe gives us many opportunities to practice what we are willing to learn! Give each person a card to write the lesson on.

Explain that at the next meeting they will start practicing facilitating an attitudinal healing group during the discussion of the lesson from *Love Is Letting Go of Fear*. Each meeting a facilitator will be chosen for each of the small groups for the next week's practice. The facilitators will open the group with a visualization and close the group. Suggest that they read the handout, "Format of Meeting and Role of Facilitator" carefully. Assign "Practice Visualizations," included in this session, as a guide for practicing visualizations in their groups.

8. Closing

Close the meeting by holding hands in a circle with a short ending or prayer such as, "We are grateful for this time together to support and care for one another."

III.   BACKGROUND INFORMATION FOR TRAINER

1. Our Role as Helpers (included in this session)

2. Excerpts from *A Course in Miracles* (included in this session)

IV.   SUGGESTED READING

Dass, Ram/Gorman, Paul. *How Can I Help?*

FORMAT OF MEETING AND ROLE OF FACILITATOR

I.   FORMAT — GROUPS BY AGE

1. Children
2. Young Adults
3. Adults

II.   TYPES OF GROUPS

1. People in crisis, i.e., affected by life-threatening illness or loss of a loved one.

2. People who want to learn the attitudinal healing model of helping in their professional work.

3. People from all walks of life and all circumstances who want to live more peacefully.

III.   FORMAT — ALL GROUPS — ROLE OF FACILITATOR

1. Read the "Prayer for Guidance," Session 1, before starting the group.

2. The facilitator may want to do the "cork" visualization. Visualize all the anxiety, anger, guilt and forgiveness draining from the top of your head through your body and being released as yellow "gucky" liquid from your toes as you take corks out of your toes. Then visualize yourself taking off your ego and hanging it on a hook outside the door before you go into your meeting.

3. Open each meeting with a visualization and meditation or ask one of the members.

4. Invite each member to talk about whatever is appropriate for the purpose of the group. Everyone should have an opportunity to share in the group at each meeting.

5. A new member brings energy to the group because they give the older members an opportunity to give their attention and love to that new person, an opportunity to help someone so they in turn can be helped.

6. The facilitator communicates with the group members if they are ill at least once between meetings, if they are scheduled bimonthly. If someone needs support between meetings, the facilitator can connect the person with another member of the group who has a similar experience.

7. Make each member aware of the meeting time and place.

8. The facilitator sends love and prayers to the members throughout the week.

9. The facilitator closes the meeting with the members holding hands in a circle

with a short statement of gratitude for their time together and to join in love. A song or music may be used for the closing.

10. The facilitator attends a monthly meeting for facilitators to discuss the programs and any personal conflicts which need resolution.

11. The facilitator reads this book before he or she facilitates a group.

IV.   FORMAT — CHILDREN'S GROUPS

1. Suggestions such as, "Introduce yourself and tell why you chose to come?" or "Describe something which made you happy this week and something that was difficult," may be used to focus the children's sharing in the beginning of the meeting.

2. Plan an activity such as art, drama, games, or puppetry for the last part of the meeting.

V.   FORMAT — ADULTS

1. Adults in crisis usually need the entire time to talk and support one another. They may choose to study the concepts in *Love Is Letting Go of Fear* or a similar text after they have met for several meetings.

2. Adult groups for personal growth as in abundant living groups for senior citizens or caregivers groups, can use the lessons in *Love Is Letting Go of Fear*, the "Essential Concepts in Attitudinal Healing" from Session 1 or similar texts for study.

VI.   PROCESS OF GROUP

1. The meditation and visualization allow the group members to experience the power of joining as One mind to release fears and guilt. The visualization is most effective when both a peaceful place and a way to discard fears and guilt are visualized.

2. The facilitator functions as an equal or peer in the group. A facilitator who is older than the participants can help by relating experiences from their child-hood. Children enjoy hearing stories about an adult's childhood. The child feels

hopeful when he sees that the adult not only survived similar experiences, but is happy.

3. The facilitator needs to allow full expression of fears and feelings. Our minds are healed when our fears are released. Members are willing to express their deepest fears when they feel understood and when their feelings or expressions are not cut off. The facilitator can trust that they will be guided to respond appropriately to people in crisis; each situation is unique.

4. The facilitator attempts to see others as they are in their eternal selves, whole and healed, and to connect with that eternal strength so that both can transcend the fear. Empathy is hearing and feeling, then transcending the fear (crisis) by seeing the other as whole and strong. Group members are helped when facilitators weep with them. Often after the tears all can sense a lifting of fear and feel hope return, and then there is resolution for both.

5. When a facilitator feels uncomfortable about a response or feeling of a member, it is important that they express the fear to the group so it can be released. The group is there for everyone to learn. If further resolution is needed, the facilitator can discuss it at the monthly facilitator meeting.

6. The facilitator does not give advice. For example, if a group member is talking about medical treatment, the facilitator needs to turn the focus on the fears connected with the treatment; for example, their fear of making a mistake.

7. When people are in crisis, the facilitator "models" the concepts (our being is our message), rather than discussing attitudinal healing concepts; they listen without judgment or comments and accept the person's feelings.

8. The facilitator encourages humor when it is appropriate. Sometimes a humorous remark can set off a chain reaction of recounting humorous experiences in the most difficult and bizarre situations, and most of the meeting will be spent in uproarious laughter. The members will remark they haven't laughed so much for months. At one family meeting where the family members met in one group, the members started telling their dreams about death. Some of the dreams were beautiful and some were hilarious. It was one of the happiest meetings ever experienced at the Center.

9. Listen to the children. They teach us about our eternal innocence.

10. Honor and trust the unique process and adaption of each person.

11. We feel peaceful when we cease to judge ourselves and others and when we are helping others.

12. When we share our fears and joys with other people who really understand, our feelings of differentness and isolation are lessened.

13. When we help another person, we help ourselves. One child said, "I forgot I was sick when I helped my friend. I feel good inside when I help someone."

DEATH AS LIFE AND GROWTH

A dream I had the night before my mother's funeral taught me to perceive death as life and growth. My mother was lying in a casket at the funeral home and all her family and friends were there. Many were sad. She suddenly sat up in her casket and angrily threw the flowers from the casket onto the floor. She got out of the casket and took her place in the first chair at the head of the family. A huge bright angel descended into the room, and wrapped his golden wings around everyone in the room. Then he ascended taking my mother with him. With his large comforting wings, the angel had also lifted the sadness of all of us there. We laughed and sang and danced in the celebration of mother's life on Earth and the new life she was beginning.

This dream reinforced my belief that God is a loving God; death is not punishment; it is a transition to another level of existence to grow. Birth and death are events within eternal life. As one of the facilitators at our Center expressed it, "At death, one just moves over to the other side."

Twenty year old Susan, who attended our young adult group at the Center, described her acceptance of her imminent transition from Earth in this way, "I am ready to go home to be with Jesus." As she neared death, she had little fear of death and almost no pain from the brain tumor which caused the end of her life on earth. I had great difficulty accepting that this talented and happy young woman would leave us. She helped teach me what Karen Schoenhols expressed in her article, "If You Should Meet a Dying Child," that in order to work effectively with the dying child, one must truly believe that God does not make any mistakes and that completeness of life is not necessarily dependent on the length of life. Susan came for a short time, but her life taught many people how to live joyfully and how to accept death.

Mary's short life ended when she was fourteen. She and her family had attended our sibling and parent's groups for one year while she was ill. Her father taught me that death is not only growth for the person who dies, but teaches us who remain on Earth. Just one month before her death, her father said to the many parents of children with life-threatening illness at our Center, "It is devastating what has happened to all of us, but before my daughter leaves, I am going to thank her for teaching me that the most important experience in life is to love." I must accept that my mind which can see only a fragment of the whole, cannot understand the reason why people leave when they are so young. All events have the purpose to teach us to love and nothing is by chance.

Children seem to know they are dying and accept that life is eternal. I sense they fear death less than adults because they are closer to birth. Many times, adults, too, sense it is time for them to leave and the meaning of life changes for them. They have accepted their death and we continue to see them as afraid when, in fact, we have projected our own fear to them. It is important to honor the person's acceptance and let him be free to leave without feeling guilty because of our need to have him stay or our fear of death.

As caretakers of ill and dying people, we need to be open to the unique needs, desires and wishes of the dying person and not judge our helpfulness by the behavior of the patient. We can trust we are always doing and saying what is appropriate and helpful when we ask for guidance. When we judge ourselves, that judgment paralyzes our ability to love.

When we love a person, we focus on the person's eternal wholeness. Only his body is in trouble. Ram Dass writes about a handicapped patient who said, "I have never ever met someone who sees me as whole. Now I understand that this is what I've got to see for myself, my wholeness." When we see an ill person as whole, we confirm our own wholeness.

When we feel whole, we feel strong and we can love and feel a unity with all others. To experience equality and connectedness with an ill person, we need to drop the models of ourselves which separate, such as nurse, teacher, loving person, so we are free simply to meet and be together. When we model what we feel rather than what we know intellectually, the sick person will sense our acceptance and love. Ram Dass expressed it this way, "My life is my message."

If we acknowledge our humanness with its feelings of both empathy and fear, we are able to help. We block our love when we feel we must be perfect models; we need to embrace our imperfections as a part of us, then we are able to accept the imperfections of the sick person. That is loving unconditionally — the love which heals fear and brings acceptance and peace.

Ill people do not feel loved when they are viewed as different; they feel separate and angry. As one young girl said, "I hate it when people are nice to me just because I am ill."

The fear of death is the fear of letting go into the unknown, the fear of being other than what we are. When we accept death as a part of our eternal adventurous journey, we can be open to the changes and opportunities to enjoy the adventure of our life. We can accept life's changes and losses as growth to an ever expanding eternal life.

Each time we are with a dying person, we resolve our own issues concerning our own death. We grow! We live more fully!

MY TEACHER, SUE

Sue was nineteen years old and had been a sophomore in college when she came to our Center in Evanston, Illinois. She had an inoperable brain tumor and her doctor had estimated she would live no more than three months. She lived for a year and she taught many people about how to live and how to die. Sue's inner being was beautiful and so was her outer. She had deep blue round eyes, a full oval face, short blonde hair and a contagious smile. She brought joy into a room just by her presence. She had been an outstanding student in high school, involved in many activities such as sports, music and cheerleading.

As weeks went by, the growth of the tumor caused paralysis in her left side. Her left arm and leg became partially paralyzed and she had to walk with a cane. Her speech was also affected. Although she could think and feel as a healthy person, she could not express herself because she could not produce the words. She would sometimes write messages awkwardly with her right hand. She always came to our young adult group at the Center. When she tried to speak, we all felt so helpless and would "feel sorry for her." She would just giggle as though it was a joke.

In February, she said she wanted to go skiing just one more time before she went "home to be with Jesus" which was the way she spoke of leaving Earth. Her wish was realized. Her parents never held her back from doing anything she thought she could do. She flew to Denver to ski. It was easier to ski than to walk. She brought back pictures in which she was skiing down a mountain in perfect balance and with so much joy.

Hospice made it possible for her to stay at home until the last two days of her life. I visited her during the last two weeks of her life. I could see her detaching herself from the world in preparation to leave. The doctors said she should be having a lot of pain and they were surprised she didn't have any. I believe it was her acceptance of death and her freedom from the fear of dying that freed her from pain.

I struggled with accepting that Sue might leave us. I thought the peace she manifested meant her physical body might be healed. To me, healing was synonymous with physical health. It seemed we were losing so much. Her life could continue to bring so much joy to the world. As Sue disengaged to be ready to leave all of us, I realized I was struggling with my own fear of death and Sue was my teacher.

Sue went to the hospital on Thursday before she died on Friday. Her brother was coming home from college. She was able to communicate with her parents and sister that she wouldn't leave until she said good-bye to her brother. He came to be with her from 10:00 to 11:00 on Friday. At 11:15 she died.

As I write this, I cry again for the loss to the world of that star of light who taught so many of us. Hundreds of people came to her memorial service — most of whom her family had never met. They came to honor her because of the joy and peace she had shared with them in life and in death.

Sue's mother came to only one more of our attitudinal healing meetings for the parents of ill children. She said for a week after Sue died, she couldn't go into her room. When she finally did go in, she sat on the bed feeling heavy with grief. As she sat there, she said it was as if a feeling of total peace descended upon her and she felt Sue's presence. She said that experience set her free of her intense grief and she felt in some way it was all right and that she could finally accept Sue's leaving.

I learned many things from Sue. I learned that healing is the replacement of fear with love and that healing can be either in life or in death. Healing is always of the mind.

I learned from Sue that healing is inner peace and is achieved through the releasing of fear so that our true natural state, which is to love, manifests. And that inner peace may be achieved in life or death. When it is achieved with death, death is the final healing.

I learned that I cannot judge or understand when or why someone's life ends on Earth. I must accept that God makes no mistakes. I also now accept that all events have a purpose, nothing is by chance.

I learned from Sue's mother that grief can be lessened when we have faith that life's events have a purpose which we often cannot understand, and that we can learn to have faith that the events in our life are to teach us to love and to transcend the darkness.

Thank you, Sue, for being my teacher!

HOW CAN I HELP?

Ram Dass & Paul Gorman

Summary by Nancy Peelen

Caring for one another, we sometimes glimpse an essential quality of our being. At times, helping happens simply in the way of things. Caring is a reflex. Expressing our innate generosity, we experience our "kin"ship, our "kind"ness. It was "Us." In service, we taste unity. Our impulses to care for one another often seem instinctive. The more we're able to act on them freely, the more opportunity we have to feel our whole impulses.

But there are clearly many ways in which we hesitate to reach out or we get confused when we try. The reasons for this don't appear to be simple at all. True compassion arises out of unity. When we break through our separateness and we meet in spirit, we experience profound moments of companionship. These, in turn, give us access to deeper and deeper levels of generosity and loving kindness.

Yet all of us seem to be born into the experience of separateness. In infancy we come to distinguish between "self" and "other." As we develop, we arrive at or devise a complex group of ideas about who we are, our ego. This includes our identity on a variety of planes in which we function simultaneously — as bodies, personalities, citizens and souls. And we have many roles to play in the course of a single day, each of which is functional and tends to call attention to itself.

For the most part, this mode of "self" or "Ego," with its individual attributes and roles, serves us in good stead. It preserves our physical and, to a degree, our psychological integrity. It gives us a sense of continuity through time, directing and documenting personal growth. It catalogues past experiences, makes available our skills, and helps keep track of capacities and limitations. Yet it is only fair to say that the quality of our helping sometimes suffers from the hold our sense of separateness might have on us. As happily and healthily as we may function within it, the degree to which we believe ourselves to be individual, isolated entities has consequences for how we care for one another.

It is to ourselves, then, that we must first look in our effort to see what limits the spontaneous expression of helping instincts. How does who we think we are affect what we have to give? How does this "delusion of consciousness" which separates us from the rest narrow the range of our compassion? So often we deny ourselves and others the full resources of our being simply because we're in the habit of defining ourselves narrowly and defensively to begin with. Less flexible, less versatile, we inevitably end up being less helpful. Any model of the self, positive or negative, will limit our capacity to help. Each form we identify with, each role we attach to, is ultimately incomplete and transient. Even if we may momentarily be secure in our chosen roles, they can still impede the quality of our service at the deepest level. Implicit in any model of who *we* think we are is a message to everyone about who *they* are. The sense of ourselves as separate is what we are contending with virtually all of the time. It's our curriculum and everybody's enrolled. How do we get on with our course of study?

1. We can become more aware of what conditioning and customs, what biases, what resistances and fears hold us back or make us hesitate.

    A. Perhaps we hold back because works of compassion have become formalized. We've already given at the office. We've already put money in the collection plate. The government would take care of it.

    B. Perhaps we've been taught "family first." Beyond a certain perimeter our standards change.

    C. Perhaps we haven't had a strong experience of family. As a result of weakened family ties, we're not quite sure of what we owe one another even in our immediate circles.

    D. Perhaps our education, our growing up, has not included the awareness of human need, helplessness, the experience of suffering. Where people live their whole lives in close proximity, there's very little choice. Suffering involves all.

    E. Perhaps it's because affluence has brought us the opportunity for privacy, the apparent power to guard against the encroachments of other people's adversity. We can isolate illness, old age, poverty and death so that we need not confront these in our daily lives.

    F. We may cling to familiar circles of association because we're afraid of being rejected. We'll help a friend who understands our sensitivities, but volunteering in unfamiliar areas might be a little threatening. They're not "us." This creates an inertia. An anxious, self-protecting ego is most comfortable in a familiar role in which it knows exactly what's expected of it. It's reluctant to grow, which means opening to the ambiguity of the unknown and learning new roles.

    G. In as much as we are caught up in any sense of personal inadequacy, we may wonder what we really can do for others, even in those moments when we're not fearful or tentative. Because we often identify ourselves, consciously or not, with our shortcomings, we may feel that we don't have enough, that we just aren't enough to help meet the needs of others. We give very little because we feel very small.

H.   We may have a difficult time facing the suffering of others because we don't know how to deal with our own pain and fear. If we're aware that it's our own pain, our own suffering, our own death that we're afraid of, our guilt may only block us further. Fear is the mind's reaction against the inherent generosity of the heart. Because the heart knows no bounds to it's giving, the mind feels called upon to define limits. Our fear is awakened not just by the suffering but by the intensity of our heart's reaction to it.

2.   What are some of the temporary defenses against the conditioning, the resistance, the bias, the fear?

A.   Denial—which often comes into play almost automatically. We try not to see, hear, or think about the suffering right before our eyes. It's as if we have an invisible screen that deflects evidence of pain as soon as it gets close enough. We delete it from awareness without even being aware that we've done so.

B.   We put some concept, idea, or label between ourselves and the suffering. Mary Jones, hurting badly, becomes Mary Jones, "schizophrenic". With a flick of the mind, we've turned a person into a problem.

C.   We try to stuff suffering into a facile spiritual or philosophical perspective. "It's just the way of things." "Suffering is part of the Grand Plan." "It's their karma." "Suffering is grace."

D.   Pity is another way we keep suffering at arm's length. We may let in a little of someone's pain, but never enough to threaten our own self-control. Pity is a controlled set of thoughts designed to assure separateness, the involuntary reflex of fear. Compassion reflects the yearning of the heart to merge and take on some of the suffering. Compassion is the spontaneous response of love.

E.   Do something. Do anything. The "we gotta" syndrome. We gotta fix this up right away. We gotta call this person for advice, get rid of some pain, call the doctor, rearrange the furniture, straighten the bed one more time. Rushing about with this reactive and zealous urgency infects the situation with a toxic tension which is the last kind of mental state anyone who's suffering needs. This agitation perpetuates itself and compounds suffering.

F.   Define boundaries of time and space for our involvement: a year off for the Peace Corps; every Tuesday morning at the battered women's shelter; eight hours a week with AIDS patients. Visit Aunt Rose in the convalescent home, but don't bring her back to the house. Careful boundaries assure that suffering won't spill over into the rest of our lives. They may be necessary; we all have other commitments. As often as not, however, they are artificially contributed to ward off that loss of control which so threatens and frightens the mind.

G. Professional roles and professional warmth. The demands of helping professionals to confront so much suffering each day are immense. Professional warmth is a survival strategy. Formal helping institutions often end up creating distances between who we think we are and those we'd like to serve. Helper is a worthy identity, yet so often it imprisons us. After all, if some of us are busy helping others, there must be others under continuous pressure to be helped. Caught in the models of the separate self, we end up diminishing one another. The more you think of yourself as a "therapist," the more pressure there is on someone to be a "patient." The more you identify as a "philanthropist" the more compelled someone feels to be a "supplicant." You are buying into precisely what people who are suffering want to be rid of: limitation, dependency, helplessness, separateness.

Back to the self. Whatever outside influences are at work, we're still asking the most basic inner question of all: Who am I? Who are we to ourselves and to one another? As we look within, we will see that to be of most service to others, we must face our own doubts, needs and resistances. We've never grown without having done so. As our inner obstacles to the expression of our caring instincts rise to the surface, we can bring them into the clear light of awareness. We can see how this resistance is affecting our ability to hear people's needs; how this habit is shaping our attitude to social action; how this expectation is contributing to burnout. By carefully observing these hindrances we can strip away some of their hidden power and reduce their influence over us.

With a certain amount of perspective, in fact, we can come to think of these not only as problems to overcome but as information leading to a deeper understanding of service. We can make use of them, helping ourselves help others.

1. We can observe our own minds at work. We can begin to see that behind all our various identities is a state of awareness that incorporates them all and yet is still able to rest behind them. As we loosen the hold of each identity so that we don't get completely lost in it, we are able to remain light and loose — able to play among these various aspects of being without identifying exclusively with any. We don't have to be anybody in particular. We don't have to be "this" or "that." We are simply free to *be*.

2. Learn to listen. Our mind is not only the source of ideas, a tool for gathering data, an instrument of training and technique, or a repository of experience and memory. Because our mind's capacity to think is so brilliant, we tend to be dazzled by it and

fail to notice other attributes and functions. There is more to the mind than reason alone. There is awareness itself and what we sometimes think of as the deeper qualities of the mind: open, quiet, receptive, reflective. Moreover, there is something we frequently experience as intuitive awareness that links us most intimately to the universe and, in allegiance with the heart, binds us together in generosity and compassion. Einstein said, "My understanding of the fundamental laws of the universe did not come out of my rational mind". Reckoning, judging, evaluating, leaping in, taking it personally, and being bored, invite us to distract and react. We are not *with* another person.

The quiet mind makes possible an overall awareness of the total situation, including ourselves. The consciousness we have access to is greater than the particular thoughts we're having or skills we've mastered. The sense of separateness falls away as we come into some deeper understanding of "It All." Whatever else we may seem to be, we're also reflections or expression of "Being," "God," "Life," the "Formless". Whatever "it" is called, there's only one of it. It's present in all creation. We ourselves are rooted in it. It is our essence. This kind of listening to the intuitive mind is a kind of surrender based on trust.

It's playing it by ear, listening for the voice within. We trust that it's possible to listen into a greater totality which offers insight and guidance.

3. Develop compassionate self-acknowledgement and acceptance. The ego may have been frightened into all kinds of defense mechanisms to control our innate generosity. But mercy and kindness were our first impulses. Natural compassion was our starting point. This may start with just simple reflection on what we're feeling. Phoniness begins to fall away. Discomfort is less toxic when it isn't denied. This quality of non-judgmental awareness not only frees us and others from the consequences of our reactivity, it allows us to enter more consciously into the experience of suffering itself. We can look at *what is*.

A dispassionate Witness is cultivated within, and the Witness is not passive, complacent, or indifferent. While not attached to a particular outcome, it's presence brings about change. This process of witnessing is dispassionate. It's open to everything so is more able to see truth. As we bring *what is* into the light of clear awareness, we begin to see that the universe is providing us with abundant clues as to the nature of the suffering before us, what is being asked, what fears have been inhibiting us, and, finally, what might really help.

Helpful Being, then is the goal. What we have to offer others will come from our sense of unity. The ego finds joy and relief in attuning to the greater Way of All Things, to the larger harmonies of the universe in which it can find its proper place and need no longer be driven by the insatiable need to control. In surrender to its proper station, the ego finds peace. The higher Self is now freer to guide the work of loving kindness and compassion. The character of service begins to change.

When you begin to see with that inner eye, that everyone has, all changes. Everyone is human, everyone is God's child. Everyone is helpless, one way or another, and everyone is helpful, too. We're all here for each other ... that is how it is.

The basic social institution is the individual human heart. It is the source of the energy from which all social action derives its power and purpose. The more we honor the integrity of that source, the more chance our actions have of reaching and stirring others. Our power will come forth from who we all are and know ourselves to be. It will be communicated in the quality of our presence, not just the substance of our message.

We're to awaken from the illusion of separateness. Common to all those habits which hinder us is a sense of separateness - we are divided within ourselves and cut off from others. Common to all those moments and actions which truly seem to help, however, is the experience of unity; the mind and the heart work in harmony, barriers between us dissolve.

Awakening from our sense of separateness is what we are called to do in all things, not merely in service. Traditions speak of us as being cut off from God, Nature, Original Mind, True Being, the Toa, the Dharma — they call on us, in one voice, to take the journey back to unity.

Service, from this perspective, is part of that journey. It is no longer an end in itself. It is a vehicle through which we reach a deeper understanding of life. Each step we take, each moment in which we grow toward a greater understanding of unity, steadily transforms us into instruments of that help which truly heals. We can, of course, help through all that we do.

At the deepest level we help through who we are. We work on ourselves in order to help others. And we help others as a vehicle for working on ourselves. On this path we will stumble, fall, and often look and feel a little foolish. We are confronting long-standing patterns of thought and action. Compassion for ourselves, perspective, humor ... they are our allies. The reward, the real grace of conscious service, then, is the opportunity not only to help relieve suffering but to grow in wisdom, experience, greater unity, and have a good time while we're doing it.

GUIDELINES - CHILDREN'S GROUPS

1. I am here to help myself by learning from you. You are my teacher and I am your teacher.

2. Each of us may use the group as a safe place to express our fears and joys.

3. When we talk about our feelings we find that each of us have the same feelings at times.

4. I am not so lonely when I talk to people who understand me because they have had the same experiences.

5. We will try to listen to each other without criticizing verbally or in our minds.

6. I will not give advice. I can tell about what helps me in a similar situation.

7. All the information talked about in the group is confidential.

8. When we release our fears to the light, love, God, we feel better.

9. I learn that I forget my problems when I listen to another person or help them.

10. When people get angry, sad, or fearful, they are asking for love.

11. Everyone has a light, love, at their hearts which can grow when they are not afraid.

GUIDELINES - ADULT GROUPS

1. We recognize we are here for our own healing and for greater inner peace.

2. We may use the group as a safe place to express our fears and joys.

3. When we risk talking about our feelings, we find common experiences which facilitate joining.

4. When we talk about our experience with people who understand us, because of our common experience, we feel connected and our loneliness is healed.

5. In the group we attempt to listen without judging.

6. Rather than give advice, we talk about what has helped us in similar experiences.

We let others find their own answers. The intention to love is enough.

7. Our relationships are equal. We are all students and teachers to each other.

8. We recognize that each of us is unique and knows him or herself better than anyone else, and that as we listen to the voice within (our intuition), we will know our own answers.

9. We learn to choose peace more often by releasing our fears and unforgiveness to the higher power, to our higher Self.

10. When we look beyond external appearances to the person within, we learn to "see" with our hearts.

11. We agree that all information shared in the group is confidential.

12. We learn that when we give love to another, we receive love ourselves.

PRACTICE VISUALIZATIONS

1. Take several deep breaths and concentrate on your breathing to center yourself and relax your mind and body. (Time) Transport yourself to a warm sunny beach where you have felt the most peaceful. See everyone here with you in a circle sitting on that beach, and feel the warmth of the sun on your body. Feel the healing light of the sun penetrate each cell of your body, and imagine it lighting up each cell. All of our bodies make a circle of light - a lighted circle which heals all fears. Take time to feel the peace. In your imagination, place into that circle of light all people you want to forgive. (Time) Return your attention to this room and let our minds join with the One Mind to be channels to send love wherever it is needed. (Time)

2. Close your eyes and get comfortable. Take three deep breaths. Imagine a beautiful summer day, clear blue sky, warm bright sun, cool breeze blowing. You are at the beach, your favorite beach. You've put the things you've brought with you down by an old log and you've taken off your shoes. The sand feels warm on your bare feet. You sit there for a moment enjoying the warmth of the sun on your back. The sound of the waves have a calming effect as they rush in and rush out. (Time)

    You relax. Now imagine that each time a wave crashes in, it pulls back with it any unpleasant thoughts you might have. Picture the waves. As you see a good sized one approaching, toss into it something you'd like to get rid of. Keep tossing until all you feel is the calmness and quietness created by the waves as they roll in and back out. Enjoy this quietness. Feel it's calm. Feel the sun on your back. (Time)

Visualize yourself back to this room. See a light in the heart center of each person in this room. That light is love. Watch it expand to cover each person's entire body until we are a circle of light. Into that circle of light, a symbol of God which heals all unforgiveness, place all those people you wish to forgive. (Time) Now let our minds be joined as One to be a channel to send love wherever it is needed. Open your eyes when you are ready.

3. Take several deep breaths to center yourself and relax your mind and body. (Time) Imagine yourself on a huge sailboat. You are sitting in a reclining deck chair on the stern of the boat. The weather is warm and you can see the reflection of the sun in the late afternoon on the calm sea. The wind is moving slowly and gently. Feel the peace. (Time)

   If you have fear thoughts you want to release, imagine them as pink clouds escaping your mind and dissipating into the atmosphere. Spend time just ebbing at peace. (Time) Now visualize all of us together sitting in a circle on the boat. Feel the love that surrounds us as a large circle of light. Let our minds unite as One Mind without limit to send love to others in the world whom we want to bless. (Time)

4. Take three deep breaths to relax your body. Relax your whole body. (Name each body part with time for one breath in between each part.) Relax your toes, ankles, calves, knees, thighs, lower torso, stomach, heart, lungs, fingers, wrists, elbows, upper arms, shoulders, neck, throat, mouth, tongue, eyes and your minds.

   In your imagination transport yourself to a tropical island beach. It is a warm sunny day. The white sand beach is lined with palm trees and tropical flowers, edged with the blue, clear, calm sea. Enjoy the beach in the way that is most peaceful for you — sitting, swimming, walking. (Time)

   Now visualize all of us sitting in a circle on the beach enjoying silent fellowship. (Time) With your eyes closed let fearful thoughts come to mind, then visualize them released from your mind as iridescent bubbles floating into the atmosphere and disappearing. (Time) Visualize yourself back to this room and open your eyes when you are ready.

OUR ROLE AS HELPERS

We were created by God to extend creation. God extended himself to his creations, us, and gave us the same loving will to create. We have been created perfect with no emptiness or lack in us. We are created whole. We cannot lose this ability to create but, can use it inappropriately by projecting or creating a dream or nightmare which does not really exist — because we think there is a lack in us.

When we created this dream, our ego self, we became fearful. This fear comes from the misperception that we can usurp the power of God and that we can separate from our Source. To believe that we have left our Source is to feel that we have left our home and that we are alone and separated from others.

Of course, we neither can nor have been able to do this, to separate and create ourselves. Since we cannot create ourselves, the errors which we think we have made in creating this ego self have never really occurred — it is impossible to make oneself. Our creation is only a dream. When we release all belief in our own ego creation of our self, we are free to know and be our real Self. This is like turning on the light and awakening from a fearful dream. The dream, our ego creation, was not true. Our ego creation is a fearful creation. When we release our fears, we awaken to our true self, the loving perfect self which is the only true creation. Our function in life is a journey back to that true self. All experiences in life enhance that journey back. It is only in relationship to others, who mirror our love and guilt, that we can learn who we are. So we must have others to share in our journey. When we see love in another, that is a mirror of our own love; when we see guilt in another, that mirrors our guilt. When we forgive another, we forgive our self.

Service is a part of the journey. It is not an end in itself. It is a vehicle by which we reach a deeper understanding of who we truly are, as we learn to forgive and love those people given to us in all of life's experiences. Those who we serve are our teachers.

No one is special. When we remember that each of us is created perfect and equal, and when we can truly see the shining radiance of all others as they were created we will remember our own perfect creation. As we remember who we really are all the errors we made in defense of our own ego creation will vanish from our minds. So we give up nothing when we let go of our ego selves; Remember that all are perfect and loved by God forever.

Nor is love special. God's love is not special. He loves all equally. *A Course In Miracles* says, "Seek not to love unlike him for there is no love apart from his." There is only one kind of love and that is God's love. When we love all persons equally, we learn to love ourselves and to experience our connection to our Source. We will experience more peace and joy as we continue our life's journey together.

OUR ROLES AS HELPERS

EXCERPTS FROM *A COURSE IN MIRACLES*

The role of teaching and learning is actually reversed in the thinking of the world. The reversal is characteristic. It seems as if the teacher and the learner are separated, the teacher giving something to the learner rather than to himself. Further, the act of teaching is regarded as a special activity in which one engages only a relatively small proportion of one's time. The course, on the other hand, emphasizes that to teach is to learn, so that teacher and learner are the same. It also emphasizes that teaching is a constant process; it goes on every moment of the day, and continues into sleeping thoughts as well.

Manual for Teachers, page 1.

A teacher of God is anyone who chooses to be one. His qualifications consist solely in this: somehow he has made a deliberate choice in which he did not see his interests as apart from someone else's. Once he has done that, his road is established and his direction is sure. A light has entered the darkness. It may be a single light, but that is enough. He has entered an agreement with God even if he does not yet believe in Him. He has become a bringer of salvation. He has become a teacher of God.

They come from all over the world. They come from all religions and from no religion. They are the ones who have answered. The Call is universal. It goes on all the time everywhere. It calls for teachers to speak for It and redeem the world. Many hear It, but few will answer. Yet it is all a matter of time. Everyone will answer in the end, but the end can be a long, long way off. It is because of this that the plan of the teachers was established. Their function is to save time. Each one begins as a single light, but with the Call at its center it is a light that cannot be limited. And each one saves a thousand years of time as the world judges it. To the Call Itself, time has no meaning.

Manual for Teachers, page 3.

Certain pupils have been assigned to each of God's teachers, and they will begin to look for him as soon as he has answered the Call. They were chosen for him because the form of the universal curriculum that he will teach is best for them in view of their level of understanding. His pupils have been waiting for him, for his coming is certain. Again, it is only a matter of time. Once he has chosen to fulfill his role, they are ready to fulfill theirs. Time waits on his choice, but not on whom he will serve. When he is ready to learn, the opportunities to teach will be provided for him.

Manual for Teachers, page 4.

Session 5

Psychological Aspects
of Grief

Session 5

PSYCHOLOGICAL ASPECTS OF GRIEF

I.   PURPOSE

1. Learn the attitudinal healing concept, "I Can Escape the World I See by Giving Up Attack Thoughts."

2. Learn the psychological aspects of grief during serious or chronic illness.

3. Learn the psychological aspects of grief from all losses.

4. Understand the feelings of a dying child.

II.   PROCEDURE

1. Visualization and meditation

Take three deep breaths to relax your mind and body. Imagine yourself slowly wandering to the edge of a small winding river. (Time) You notice the beautiful surroundings and feel the warmth of the sun. You hear the trickling of the water over the rock bottom. (Time) Imagine your fears and troubles are pebbles on the bank. Pick them up one by one and toss them into the river and watch them flowing away. (Time) As you turn to look, we have all joined you. We form a circle and are joined as One in one purpose to send healing, joyful love to all who need it. When you are ready, open your eyes.

End with the "Prayer for Guidance."

2. Lesson

Ask a participant to read lesson 5, page 85, "I Can Escape the World I See by Giving Up Attack Thoughts," in *Love Is Letting Go of Fear*. Invite each person to relate an experience in which this lesson helped them to experience something more peacefully or when it might have helped them if they had remembered to use it.

3. Loss and grief

Read "Emotional Stress and Grief," included in this session. Discuss the experience of grief for a seriously or chronically ill person. Read and discuss "Loss and Grief" and Kubler-Ross' "Stages of Dying" included in this session. These articles explain that life is a series of losses, some developmental and some extreme, all of which cause grief and require adaptation in a lesser or greater degree. From all of these experiences with loss, grief, adaptation or acceptance, we can learn to let go of our worldly concerns, our fears, and replace them with love, which is the final healing.

Read and discuss "If I Should Meet a Dying Child", written by Karen Schoenhals. This article explains how we can understand a dying child and how we can learn from their wisdom as they near death. The children become our teachers.

4. Guest speaker

Invite someone who works with people in grief due to illness or loss of a loved one to speak to the group about the psychological aspects of grief.

5. Assignment

Assign lesson 6, page 91, "I Am Not the Victim of the World I See", in *Love Is Letting Go of Fear*. Ask each person to write it on a card.

Explain that next week the subject will be "Using Your Imagination": how art, music, meditation and visualization can be used to express feelings. Ask each participant to bring a written description of a visualization which could be used for a children's group or one appropriate for an adult group. They can be typed and given to each member for their use with groups.

Suggest that in creating the visualization, it is important to have a peaceful place, a place to discard fears, and a place to be together as a group at the ending. Sometimes it is not appropriate to use the training visualization recommended ending "... minds joined as One without limit, etc..." Your intuition will tell you what is appropriate. REMEMBER TO ASK. Do not describe too many details. People have their own visions of a beautiful beach, woods or mountains, so let them image their own. Be sure to allow time for quiet because that is when the peace can be felt and fears released. Too many words interrupt the flow of feelings in the group members.

6. Closing

Close the meeting by standing and holding hands in a circle and with a statement such as, "We are thankful for this time we have had together to love and support one another".

III.   BACKGROUND INFORMATION FOR TRAINER

"Healing, Remission and Miracle Cures," Brendan O'Regan (Resource section)

IV.   SUGGESTED READING

Kubler-Ross, Elisabeth. *On Children and Death.*

EMOTIONAL STRESS AND GRIEF DURING ILLNESS

Mary Hellstern, a counselor, spoke to our training group at the Center in Evanston. She had been crippled from muscular dystrophy for many years. When I first knew her, she walked with crutches and in four years she was confined to a wheelchair. Her office and home were in a high-rise apartment building in downtown Chicago where she lived alone. She could park her car in an underground garage, manipulate her wheelchair and get herself into the elevator and up to her fifth floor apartment.

Although I knew she suffered grief as she lost her physical abilities, I never experienced her as a depressed person. I asked her how she sustained a happy, hopeful attitude, for the most part, in spite of her losses and frustrations. Her reply was that although she couldn't control her physical problems, she could choose her attitude and she wouldn't cheat herself by being unhappy!

She spoke to us about the psychological aspects and emotional stresses due to illness from her personal experience. She said that when you are first told about a serious illness, you fear loss of control, loss of competence and loss of life; you feel inadequate, helpless and vulnerable. She explained that each time she experienced a greater loss, as when she went from the crutches to the wheelchair, all of these fears became intensified and had to be dealt with and adapted to.

The levels of feelings of adaptation are first shock, then denial, anger, depression, bargaining and acceptance. Some people do not experience these feelings in this order; some move back and forth in the levels and others skip a level or more. Specific fears which accompany the feelings are the fear of rejection, fear of pain, fear of failure and fear of death. Mary explained that in severe illness, three of these fears are felt at the same time; that is why the feelings are so intense.

Since society values "doing" versus "being," when the ill person cannot "do" any more, they feel rejected and a failure. Again, she urged us to remember the concept that our value is already established by God; we are his creation and our value cannot be limited by others or our own value judgments. When we believe we are valuable just because we exist, our beliefs are not affected by what happens to us, i.e. our environment. We can see value beyond a difficult experience and losses, we can choose whether to laugh or cry.

She said that both the ill person and the people who are caring for, or being with the person need to have a sense of what they're afraid of. When we can label our fears and accept them rather than deny them, we dissipate their intensity. When we are not aware of our real fears, or deny them, we cannot relate honestly to another person. This causes feelings of separation and loneliness. When we acknowledge our fear, our behavior toward the other person can be congruent with our thoughts and feelings and our feelings of separation are healed.

When someone in our family is sick both the sick person and family member fear a change in the relationship and that change is a loss that must be adapted to by everyone. The well person feels insecure because the sick person is no longer strong and able to give support, and the sick person is looking to the well person hoping for continued strength and support.

One evening, when Mary got out of her car with a lap full of books, the books fell to the garage floor. Through her tears of frustration, she saw the custodian coming to pick them up. As she thanked him profusely because she thought she was imposing on him, he said "Don't thank me, lady, I want to thank you. I never get a chance to pick up anything except garbage so it is my joy to pick up your books." This incident demonstrates the importance of our being able to receive love so people can have the joy of giving.

LOSSES AND GRIEF

Mary Hellstern spoke about the fears and losses experienced by people with serious or chronic illnesses. Fears are always the result of losses or the fear of losses. When we have any loss, or fear a loss, we grieve. Life is a succession of worldly losses and continuous adaptation. Some losses are extreme, as with serious illnesses, and difficult to accept, and others are so gradual we adapt more easily. The gradual losses are natural losses we experience, as when our children leave home, our physical energy decreases with age, our spouse dies and we are old, facing death.

The elderly woman, for example, usually must adapt to the loss of her role as a needed mother, perhaps the loss of her husband,, the loss of unfulfilled dreams, perhaps the loss of her children being nearby, sometimes the loss of her home, and her impending loss of physical life.

A child with a life-threatening illness needs to adapt more quickly to even greater losses. He needs to adapt to the loss of physical energy, loss of competence, loss of control, loss of his peer group, loss of his healthy place in the family, often the loss of his role in school, sometimes the loss of his physical attractiveness and perhaps the loss of life.

Whether the losses are developmental or extreme, grieved people will experience to a lesser or greater degree all or some of the levels of adaptation: shock, denial, anger, depression, bargaining and acceptance. With all losses and grief we experience to some degree the same fears: loss of control, loss of competence, loss of freedom, failure, pain and rejection. We feel inadequate, helpless and vulnerable.

All of life's changes, whether developmental or extreme, are felt as losses and require adaptation or we become inflexible, angry, unhappy people. We can choose to accept and learn that all of life's losses have a purpose, and teach us to let go of our worldly (ego) attachments (fears), so that fear can be replaced with love. Then we finally know our real Self is spirit and eternal — the final healing.

Knowing the normal process of grieving helps us to be patient with ourselves as we experience losses in our lives, and to be patient with the people the Universe sends us as our students and teachers.

When a grieving person comes to us for help, how can we help? We always need to remember we are here to love, not to change others. We can only change ourselves. So really all we can do is love. To love is to accept unconditionally the feelings of the grieved person, to listen without judgment, and to finally transcend our mutual feelings of sadness by visualizing the person's eternal wholeness and strength.

Remember, we cannot judge the outcome of our help. Our help is given with the intent to share and give love. Giving and receiving are the same as we experience that giving love to another is the same as receiving love.

The following is from Duba, Deborah, *Coming Home: A Guide to Dying at Home with Dignity*, page 141. Aurora Press, Inc. 205 Third Ave. 2A, NY, NY, 10003, 1987. Available from: Aurora Press, P.O. Box 573, Santa Fe, New Mexico 87504 (505) 989-9804. (Used by permission)

ELISABETH KUBLER-ROSS'
STAGES OF DYING

Elisabeth Kubler-Ross, a Swiss-born doctor and author, has served us all with great love. Her work with dying people and the attitude she brings to dying have given many people all over the world the courage to look at a part of our lives that we've not faced before. Working with hundreds of patients, she noted a process that most go through as they die. Most people don't consciously want to die and this process is the way in which they make peace with this change.

The stages — denial and isolation, anger, bargaining, depression and acceptance — are a **process**, not a goal. It's the same process many of us go through in facing any loss. Not all people go through all the stages; some skip stages and others move back and forth between them, sometimes from moment to moment.

The following description of the stages is just a clue to feelings you and the dying person may have. If our choice is to let people die in their own way, there's no need to push them through the stages to acceptance. A person can die with dignity even if he or she never accepts dying.

Denial and isolation. Dr. Kubler-Ross calls this the "No, not me" stage. It appears in the beginning of a life-threatening illness and often reappears many times. "It can't be true." The patient may shop around for different doctors or treatments. She or he may not want to "talk about it" or may want to be alone or with people who don't know what's happening. Shock and numbness are common. Dr. Kubler-Ross suggests that we just be there lovingly when a person is denying and let them know, "When you want to talk I'm available."

A person may need denial to cope with impending death, to adjust to losses already experienced and to tolerate suffering and pain. Some die in denial — that's their way. As family and friends we may also experience denial. Check to see if the denial is yours or the dying person's.

Anger. The "Why me?" stage. Rage, envy, resentment. Anger at losing control. The anger is randomly projected, often on innocent people. "You don't love me." "The doctors and nurses are incompetent." "Goddamn, God!" Dr. Kubler-Ross suggests we not respond with nasty criticism or kill them with kindness. Better to rub it in. Affirm what's happening: "Doesn't it make you mad?" "Don't you feel like screaming?" The relief from venting anger may move the person toward greater acceptance of what is happening.

Sometimes the most loving things we can do for a dying person (or people with a part of themselves dying) is to be a target for an outburst of anger. It's not hard to do if we **don't take it personally** and remember that expressing anger often helps a person move toward accepting dying. I'm not suggesting, however, that you be a "patsy" for any angry bully.

It's OK to feel scared if the person yells at you and it's OK to be angry with God.

Imagining yourself in their place may help you understand. You'd be angry too!

Bargaining. The "Yes, me but ..." stage. "It's OK for me to die if Eve and I can just take a trip to Hawaii first." "If I can just live 'til the kids graduate ..." "If I live, I'll dedicate my life to God." Bargaining is a temporary truce. The patient may seem peaceful. It's a good time to take care of wills and other business. Dr. Kubler-Ross notes that very few people keep their bargains if they do live longer.

Depression is the womb in which a new choice or way of being grows. It's caused by holding on to someone or something we can't have or by holding in some feelings we haven't expressed -- anger, sadness, guilt, even love. Robert Waterman of Southwestern College of Life Sciences in Santa Fe, calls one form of depression "trapped love." "We feel depressed when we block ourselves from receiving or expressing the living love that we are."

Depression is useful for a dying person and family holding on to a body. Making a change or letting go eventually becomes more desirable than the greyness of depression. You may be able to help someone see which feeling needs expressing.

Acceptance. "It's OK." stage. Quiet, at peace, neither depressed nor angry. Dr. Kubler-Ross describes it as "time to contemplate the coming end with a certain degree of quiet expectation." The person is probably sleeping more; his or her concerns no longer relate to the outside world. It is "the final rest before a long journey." This period may be almost void of feeling. You can be there quietly, reassuringly. Again, resignation (giving up) is not the same as acceptance.

Our response to dying is like any other big decision we make in our lives. We can go from acceptance, having made a decision, back to bargaining or questioning that decision. It's very helpful to look for these stages in ourselves as well as in the dying person we love. It's important for the family to arrive at acceptance so their desire to prolong life doesn't contradict the patient's wish to die in peace. It's easier if we feel acceptance when we bring someone home, even if this feeling changes many times.

IF YOU SHOULD MEET A DYING CHILD
Karen Schoenhals

The following is an excerpt from an article which appeared in *Evangelizing Today's Child*, Volume 8, N6, 1981.

"And the gold one stands for Heaven," announced six-year-old Rebecca with an air of serene enthusiasm that scarcely could be missed.

It was not coincidental that Becky had chosen the final page of *Wordless Book* to present to the primary class that Sunday morning. For the past two months, Becky had been preoccupied with the subject of Heaven and had eagerly shared her innermost thoughts with the entire class. "Heaven" had become the subject which overshadowed the content of every lesson and this Sunday was no exception.

"I'm going there ..." she concluded with a sense of immediacy that could not be ignored.

Not understanding why, but feeling compelled to follow the lead of her young student, Mrs. P. laid aside her prepared lesson and led the children in a moving discussion about death and what it will be like to go to Heaven and be with Jesus.

Mrs. P. was deeply saddened, but not surprised the following Saturday morning when she learned that Becky had taken ill during the night and had, indeed, gone to be with Jesus.

"It's all right," she sighed with a feeling of confidence. "Somehow Becky knew she was going; Becky had talked about her death and she was ready."

Whether in light of a diagnosed terminal illness or, at times, when facing sudden loss of life, children after the age of three are aware of their own impending death. According to Dr. Elisabeth Kubler-Ross, the well-known Swiss psychiatrist who has done extensive counselling with terminally ill children, "Because children do not repress their feelings, it is not a question of whether they know; it is a question of whether they are willing to share with you." (Kubler-Ross, E., seminar on Death and Dying, November, 1980.)

Perhaps God will involve you in a spiritual ministry to the dying child. As a Christian, your overall goal would be to share the love of God and offer the hope of eternal life as the answer to the problem of human death. In moving toward this goal, it is important that you become familiar with some of the issues with which the child is struggling. You need to develop communication skills which will enable the child to share his feelings with you.

Dealing with the subject of death is difficult for all of us, especially when considering death on a personal level. In a society that stresses youth, beauty, gratification, death is viewed as the "grim reaper" coming in unexpectedly, often robbing one of a long and pleasure-filled life. For the Christian, death is the very essence of life. Yet, even for the Christian, death involves the disappointment of unfulfilled dreams, the pain of separation, the crippling feelings of guilt and the devastation of loneliness and loss.

A commonly held belief today is that the person who dies at an early age has been cheated out of life and, in response, people experience feelings of anger toward God for allowing such an injustice to occur. It is necessary to be able to understand these feelings even though such a belief is not in keeping with the Christian concept that God is a God of love who has a perfect plan for each of His Children.

In order to work effectively with the dying child, one must truly believe that God does not make any mistakes and that completeness of life is not necessarily dependent on length of life. In addition, one must be comfortable with the reality of his own death and must have worked through unresolved personal issues around death, dying and loss. Even so, there will scarcely be a more vigorous test of your Christian faith than dealing with the death of a child.

Regardless of whether the child has been informed of the seriousness of his illness or not, he is at some level, aware of his prognosis and desperately needs to share his feelings about what is happening to him. Parents, overwhelmed by their feelings of grief often are psychologically unavailable to listen to the feelings and meet the emotional needs of their child.

TO COMMUNICATE

A major challenge in working effectively with the dying child involves learning to communicate in a helpful manner. The problem in getting the child to share his feelings is that the feelings he is experiencing are too painful to share. From the ages of four to twelve, children experiencing emotional pain do not convey their messages directly; rather they use non-verbal symbolic language to tell you about their dying. Messages are most often conveyed through playing with dolls and stuffed animals, through drawings and pictures and through creative story telling. Although older children and adolescents are more likely to communicate directly, they often resort to symbolic verbal messages such as speaking in hypothetical terms and to acting out their feelings through their behavior. (Kubler-Ross, Macmillan, 1981.)

For the child, facing death involves a head-on encounter with two of the most powerful fears of childhood; fear of separation from parents and fear of bodily mutilation. In addition, around the age of five, the child begins to sense a need for control over what is happening to him. At this time, the child's perception of death begins to emerge as a catastrophic force bearing down upon him over which he has no power. Symbolic messages most often convey these prominent fears and the feelings of helplessness that accompany them; such feelings are far too frightening to convey directly.

Talking about one's feelings is a person's best way of mastering them. Remember that feelings do not always make sense and they may not be based on reality. You cannot argue a person out of what he is feeling.

Helpful communication is not geared towards supplying answers to make the person feel better.

Asking the child to draw a picture of himself in his world can be a non-threatening way to encourage expression of feelings. Dr. Kubler-Ross (Macmillan, 1981) describes the use of spontaneous art as a means of the child communicating his knowledge of his illness and impending death — even the knowledge of when death will occur.

Session 6

Using Your Imagination

Session 6

USING YOUR IMAGINATION

I.   PURPOSE

1. Learn the concept, "I Am Not the Victim of the World I See."

2. Create and guide a visualization.

3. Experience the release of fears through a meditation with music.

4. Learn visualizations created by children.

5. Discuss how visualizations can help children and adults release fears.

6. Experience drawing as a way of releasing blocks to love.

II.   PROCEDURE

1. Meditation and visualization

In this visualization the participants will experience music as a medium to help open their hearts to receive love.

Play a recording of music which symbolizes energy, vitality and growth. Ask the members to take three deep breaths to relax their minds and bodies. Suggest they observe themselves in this visualization as if they are watching a movie:

See yourself lying on the ground in a fetal position. Imagine you are a seed in the earth. Feel the music moving through the soil like water, nourishing you, helping you grow. Let the music begin moving you; feel yourself flowing toward the sunlight. Moving as slowly as you wish, gradually rise into a standing position, in the sunlight, unfolding more and more into a joyous being.

Now ask that all minds be joined as one mind with the Christ Mind without limit to send love to the world to where it is needed.

End with the "Prayer for Guidance."

2. Visualizations created by group members

Ask the group members to close their eyes as they listen to the visualizations written by the group members. Suggest that one-half of them be read now and the other half at the end of this meeting. Give a copy of the visualizations to the group members for their resource files.

3. Lesson

Read "I Am Not the Victim of the World I See," from *Love Is Letting Go of Fear*, page 91, and ask each person to relate an experience in which the concept helped to bring more peace to their life. Form smaller groups and practice facilitating.

4. Visualizations

Discuss "Visualizations," included in this session, which describes how people use visualizations.

5. Visualizations created by children

Read and discuss "Visualizations Created by Children" included in this session.

6. Art exercise

Introduce the art exercises and guide the exercise as described in the "Releasing Blocks to Love Through Art" included in this session.

7. Assignments

Explain to the members that the subject of the next two sessions is "Forgiveness." The next meeting will be a discussion of the attitudinal healing concept of forgiveness and the following session they will experience an exercise in forgiveness. Ask each person to write about what forgiveness means to them to be used in the discussion.

Assign "Today I Will Judge Nothing that Occurs," page 97, in *Love Is Letting Go of Fear*, and write it on a card.

8. Closing

Close the meeting by asking everyone to close their eyes and relax their minds to listen to the last half of the visualizations contributed by the members.

End the meeting with the statement, "We are happy we could be together tonight."

III. SUGGESTED READING

1. Achterberg, Jeanne. *Imagery in Healing*.

2. Cousens, Norman, M.D. *Anatomy of An Illness*.

3. Crandall, Joanne. *Self-Transformation Through Music*.

4. Edwards, Betty. *Drawing on the Right Side of the Brain*.

5. Matthews-Simonton, Stephanie, Simonton, O. Carl, M.D. and Creighton, James L. *Getting Well Again*.

6. O'Regan, Brendan. "Healing, Remission and Miracle Cures."

7. Seigel, Bernard, M.D. Love, Medicine and Miracles.

8. The children at the Center for Attitudinal Healing, Tiburon, California. *There Is a Rainbow Behind Every Dark Cloud*.

9. The children at the Center for Attitudinal Healing, Tiburon, California. *Another Look At the Rainbow*.

VISUALIZATIONS CREATED BY CHILDREN

Children like to create their own visualizations for many purposes. They can visualize themselves happy and free of fears. For example, they may create visualizations to participate in the healing of their bodies and to distract them during painful or fearful medical procedures. Imagery may be used to release any fears, such as anger, attack thoughts, fear of rejection, feelings of loneliness, fear of failure, fear of physical disability, fear of being "different" and fear of death.

Gary, one of the children from the Tiburon Center on the TV film "Donahue and Kids," is an example of how a child participates in helping heal his body. He saw his brain tumor as a meat ball and he visualized space ships attacking it with lasers blasting off chunks until it was destroyed. During chemotherapy treatment, children can visualize the chemotherapy attacking and killing off the diseased cells.

One of the children in our Evanston Center group visualized the place on her arm where the needle would be inserted during medical treatment as a marshmallow which was insensitive to pain.

Another child told about how she visualized planning and doing her school work when she was getting intravenous chemotherapy, to distract her from the pain.

The children at the Tiburon Center created the "garbage can" visualization. It is used by many centers to open both adult and children's groups. The group members visualize a large brown garbage can. One by one, they slowly place all their angry thoughts and fears into the garbage can. A large yellow helium-filled balloon has been tied to the lid and it lifts the can into the sky. Farther and farther, up and up it goes, until it and all the fears it contains are out of sight and their minds are free of those fearful thoughts.

Two other visualizations the children have created can be helpful also to adults who enjoy a vivid imagination. They visualize a little elevator parked just above their hearts, and in that elevator is a little man in a red jacket with a very small red toolbox. This elevator can travel anywhere in the body where there is pain just by thinking it there. If the pain is in your stomach, for example, the elevator slowly descends to exactly the right place. Then, the little man in the red jacket opens the door, exits the elevator with his little red toolbox and fixes the pain. Finally, he ascends back to his place just above the heart where he stays all the time, waiting to fix pain.

In another visualization, the children pretend they have a pink plastic bucket full of warm water with soap bubbles. They pretend they take out their brains which have dirty places caused by anger and fear. They gently dunk the brain in and out of the soft, sudsy water until it is all pink and clean again, and then they put the brain back in, having washed away all the grimy thoughts that made them unhappy.

VISUALIZATIONS

To visualize is to create. Before an artist creates a work of art, he visualizes. When an inventor creates an invention, he visualizes. When a scientist learns something new, it comes as an image before he can concretize it. When an architect designs a building, he visualizes first.

In the same way, we are architects of our lives. We can visualize life experiences and attitudes which bring joy to ourselves and those around us or we can create a life which feels fearful and hopeless. Each day we choose.

Clement Stone, an industrialist, and Earl Nightingale, a philosopher, write about the importance of visualizing the experiences which will bring happiness into our lives. They write about the self-fulfilling prophecy concept; the belief that our thoughts alter our life experience. If we expect happiness, we will be happy; if we expect problems, our life will manifest unhappy events. We attain the quality of experience we anticipate and visualize.

People of all ages choose to create visualizations for many purposes. When I became angry at the behavior of my children when they were young, I would remember each one's face at their most happy time and I would transfer that face onto their unhappy face and then ask to be released of my anger. That would dissipate the anger and help me remember how much I loved them and how lovable they really were.

I now use this same visualization to release difficult encounters. We use it also to help us remember that eternal reality — that joyous face — of the people in our groups who are depressed or who are physically ill. We then ask that our eternal mind be connected with the other person's eternal mind so that both our minds may be free of fear and free to love.

Bob was a fourth grade boy who was transferring to our school at the beginning of fifth grade. He was reading at middle second grade level. His school recommended he be placed back in fourth grade when he came to us the following year. I sensed that he was a highly capable child and suggested he be placed in fifth grade which was his desire also. I totally ignored his past school records and suggested to his parents that every morning and evening they visualize him as he had been at his happiest moment and release themselves of their perceptions of his past performance. By spring of his fifth grade, he tested middle seventh grade on his reading scores and he had learned to value himself as a worthy child intellectually and socially.

Children are often affected by our prophecy of their future based on their past behavior. Our vision of them becomes their prophecy for themselves. Craig was a nine year old fourth grade boy who was considered the biggest problem in his school by the entire staff. He could not control his anger at home or at school; he hit and kicked children in the classroom, on the playground and when he was walking to and from school. He was failing in school because he could not concentrate to finish his work. He had given up; he had no friends. He was seeing a counselor and his family was cooperating in every way to help him.

The family was transferred to Florida. The principal of his new school was a wise man who understood children need to be released from people's past perceptions of them to be free to see themselves as worthwhile, adequate, loving and lovable children.

He chose to shelve Craig's thick file so his new teacher could not judge her new student by his past. His teacher then perceived him as a good, cooperative student and welcomed him into her classroom.

Craig became that happy child he wanted so much to be and as he was perceived to be by the staff at his new school. He was a good student in all ways and made many friends throughout his school career, through college. He is a lesson in remembering there is no past, that we cannot judge, and that the past is and this moment is the only time there is.

O. Carl Simonton, M.D., in his book, *Getting Well Again*, discusses the effect of imaging a positive outcome to illness as opposed to a negative outcome. For example, a patient who visualizes that he will be well again experiences hope in his life and cooperates in the medical treatment. The patient who visualizes a negative outcome will experience hopelessness and believe that nothing will help him recover.

John, a sixty-five year old airline captain, used visualization to help in healing his illness. He was diagnosed with a serious melanoma. He told about being in the oncologist's office where he met a six year old boy who was in remission from cancer. The little boy told him he would get well if he would visualize the "good" cells eating up the "bad" cells at least twice daily. The pilot faithfully followed the little boy's advice. John has been in remission for five years now and he believes the imagery is responsible for his healing. What a wonderful lesson in learning that we are equal regardless of age and that we are all both students and teachers to each other!

RELEASING BLOCKS TO LOVE THROUGH ART

INTRODUCTION:

1. Meditation and visualization are experiences of images while in an alpha state — a condition of the mind when it is quieted and focused inward.

2. Imagination is a facet of this experience.

3. Artists - literary, visual, dramatic, musical - tap into imagination (while the mind is in an alpha state) to visualize or "auralize" an idea before they create. We all do this, *but* our lack of technical training *or* our fear of that lack short-circuits the flow from mind to material.

EXAMPLE: Children, until third-fourth grade, exhibit an uninhibited flow of drawings, constructions, dramas, tales, etc. At about eight or nine years old, most students become very critical of their own products. Inhibited, now most stop creating. Their imaginings (visualizations) stay inside. They are afraid of the judgment of the physical product that results from their wonderful visualization. (Some theorize that this occurs due to the left hemispheres developing strength which increasingly overpowers the right hemisphere - the creative, daydreaming side.)

PREPARATION:

1. I want now to do a visualization/meditation during which I will suggest specific emphasis. When we are finished, I will ask that you depict your image on paper.

   To help dispel your fear, be assured that you do not have to share your product. Your drawing is for your benefit — your experience is your release and sharing is not necessary. The purpose of creation is the catharsis and joy that results for you. Sharing it often overwhelms the benefit of expression. If sharing heightens your experience then we all will enjoy that opportunity.

2. Arrange materials at your side.

VISUALIZATION:

Relax your body in your chair. Feel yourself let go of tension as you breathe slowly and deeply three times.

See yourself entering a room where you find great relaxation. You are there alone. As you cross the room to the most comfortable chair, notice how the light in the room reflects a peaceful atmosphere. Notice the glow that enhances the shapes and colors surrounding you. Allow your body to relax in the chair you've chosen. As you sit there with your eyes closed, listen to the subtle, friendly sounds in the room.

From outside the room you hear footsteps approaching the entrance to your room. As the footsteps get closer, you turn your attention to the door and anticipate another person entering your space.

As the door opens, you see a person with whom you feel great conflict. As that person moves closer to you, you notice how the atmosphere seems to have changed. Notice the sounds now. Notice the colors and shapes around you. Notice the vibrations that fill the air around the two of you and between the two of you.

Now remember from deep inside your heart center a love that you have for all people. Call that love forward to engulf the two of you with understanding for each other. Let the love flow over the intensity between you and smooth it -- resolve it. Let the love radiate out to fill the space around and between you. Feel how the conflict shrinks. See it growing smaller ... smaller ... until it is gone. Love now fills that place that the conflict occupied. As you enjoy a feeling of oneness with that person, see the color of your love, the color of the room. Notice how the shape between you has changed. Memorize all your impressions. Give your loving thoughts to your friend. See them flow from your eyes and your smile to and around your friend.

Hold onto these impressions that you have. Remember all of them that you have felt in this room. Choose one that is very strong, and bring it back with you as you re-enter this reality. Wake up slowly and position your paper and pen in hand. Allow your impressions to flow from your special room to your hand and to your paper.

Cheryl Poole
Consultant for Gifted Education
Allegan Intermediate School District

Session 7

Forgiveness Workshop

Session 7

FORGIVENESS WORKSHOP

I. PURPOSE

1. Learn the concept, "Today I Will Judge Nothing that Occurs," from *Love Is Letting Go of Fear*.

2. Learn the attitudinal healing concept of "forgiveness."

3. Experience "forgiveness" through the unconditional love of the group members.

II. PROCEDURE

1. Meditation and visualization

Open the meeting with the following visualization to help the members relax their bodies and free their minds so they are able to give and receive love, and to learn they are loving and lovable people.

Take two deep breaths to relax. (Time) Relax your whole body. (Name each body part with time for one breath in between each part.) Ask them to relax their toes, ankles, calves, knees, thighs, lower torso, stomach, heart, lungs, fingers, wrists, elbows, upper arms, shoulders, neck, throat, mouth, tongue, eyes and their minds.

Continue the visualization as follows:

In your imagination, transport yourself to a tropical island beach. It is a warm sunny day. The white sand beach is lined with palm trees and tropical flowers edge the blue, clear, calm sea. Enjoy the beach in the way that is most peaceful for you, by sitting, swimming, walking. (Time)

Now visualize all of us sitting in a circle on the beach enjoying silent fellowship. (Time) With your eyes closed let fearful thoughts come to mind and visualize them being released from your mind like iridescent bubbles floating into the atmosphere and disappearing. (Time) Let our minds be joined as One with the Christ Mind without limit to send love to all those in the world who need love. (Time) When you are ready, turn your attention to the room.

End with the "Prayer for Guidance."

2. **Lesson**

   Read and discuss lesson 7, "Today I Will Judge Nothing that Occurs," page 97 of *Love Is Letting Go of Fear*, and ask each person to relate an experience in which this concept taught them to perceive a situation with peace rather than conflict. Practice facilitating in small groups.

3. **What does "forgiveness" mean?**

   Ask each group member to read what they have written about what forgiveness means to them at the present time. Explain that forgiveness can be experienced in different ways. The discussion for today will focus on the attitudinal healing concept of forgiveness described in this book.

4. **"Forgiveness"**

   Give each member a copy of "Forgiveness" included in this session. Discuss the concept of forgiveness as described on this page.

5. **Assignment**

   Assign lesson 8, "This Instant is the Only Time There Is," page 105 in *Love is Letting Go of Fear*, for the following week. Write the lesson on cards.

6. **Closing**

   Close the meeting by standing in a circle holding hands with a brief sentence such as "We are grateful for this time we have been together to listen to and support one another."

III. **BACKGROUND INFORMATION FOR TRAINER**

   Excerpts from *A Course in Miracles*, (included in this session).

IV. **SUGGESTED READING**

   1. Hay, Louise. *You Can Heal Your Life.*

   2. Stauffer, Edith R., Ph.D. *Unconditional Love and Forgiveness.*

FORGIVENESS

To forgive is to let go of our past. All grievances have to do with the past. Grievances are fears; so to forgive is to let go of our fears. Our attitude is healed when we forgive.

The only eternal reality is LOVE. When we forgive ourselves, others, and the world that is, and release our fears, we are aware of our loving and lovable self and we experience greater inner peace. Forgiveness then becomes our most important function. When we forgive we are free to experience our true divine Self and to know we are joined with the all other divine Selves in One Mind with God. As each of us achieves greater inner peace, that peace is extended to all the world because we belong to the One Mind.

The process of releasing our fears is complex and usually takes a period of time. Since our physical, emotional and spiritual development are all processes, we have layers of fears which need to be understood. As we release layers of our fears, we achieve a deeper and deeper understanding and we are finally free to love. No one in the world escapes fears but everyone can label them, reconsider their causes, learn to evaluate them as only learning experiences, embrace them and release them.

Our fears have accumulated since our birth and come from many experiences and misperceptions. Many of our fears are repressed or denied. Often social conditioning has taught us to believe we are valued because of our good behavior and accomplishments. We are taught certain standards of behavior are acceptable and others are not. We are punished by a higher authority — our parents, teachers, employers, etc. — for the unacceptable behavior and often rewarded for the "good" behavior. We are socialized then to evaluate in terms of "good" and "bad," acceptable and unacceptable, correct and incorrect, ugly and attractive, rich and poor, successful and unsuccessful, and so on. We perceive ourselves as being judged by external forces and controlled by them.

When we perceive ourselves as being judged by external powers, we are in conflict because our behavior may be judged "good" by one authority and "bad" by another. When we feel external judgments control us, we blame other people or experiences for our behavior. When we are judged by conflicting standards we respond with inconsistent behavior. This causes us to feel guilty because we are violating our personal integrity.

We also fear punishment for that "bad" behavior. To alleviate the guilt and fear of punishment, we blame others for our "bad" behavior. So you can see that when we are able to forgive the projected guilt, "bad" behavior of another person, we are forgiving our own "bad" behavior.

When we perceive that external judgments are controlling our behavior, we find ourselves behaving in ways which are not congruent with how we feel. That makes us feel dishonest and again, guilty.

Experiences from birth and very early childhood which are no longer in our conscious memory and which may have been denied or repressed because they were so painful add to the complexity of understanding our fears.

Another reason we deny or repress fears which make us feel guilty is because we are afraid of being punished by God. Because our mind is conditioned to believe that punishment by an authority is inevitable if we have done something "wrong," and because some of us have been taught the concept of a punishing God, we fear that God will punish us.

When we commit to having inner peace as our goal and forgiveness as our function, we are asking to have revealed to us what needs to be forgiven. We will be shown in ways limited only by our fears of the unknown. We will be shown through relationships with friends, family, group members, children, teachers and strangers. We will be shown through dreams and perhaps images in meditation. We will learn from the sciences, nature, and the writings of aware teachers from all paths from ancient times to the present time. We may learn from travel to other parts of the world, from stage productions, television and movies. We also learn directly through our higher self, our intuition, our inner voice.

A series of images during mediation helped me to understand my fears and the process of forgiveness. I saw a very large snake; he represented my fears. He crawled behind a log to hide. His hiding symbolized my hidden, repressed and denied fears. In front of his head and at the end of the log appeared a large cage. The snake then became many animals — an alligator, birds, a boa constrictor, fox, a skunk. These animals had appeared in previous dreams to represent specific fears. For example, the fear I experienced when my mother told me secrets when I was a small child was symbolized by a skunk under the porch. Times when I didn't tell the whole truth so I could have my way or cover a mistake were symbolized by a fox. Each animal was specific to some experience when I felt fear or guilt.

As the animals scampered into the cage, I perceived them differently, as pets. I embraced them. The cage door was open and they were free to leave. The cage symbolized the restrictions our fears place on our living and being. When my fears were released, the snake no longer existed; it was transformed into a log.

After the animals left, I saw in the back of the cage what I perceived as a ferocious lion. He paced back and forth and finally walked out of the cage and quietly laid down on the sand in the sun outside the cage door. The lion is a symbol of God to me. He rested peacefully with both eyes closed waiting for me to accept him. He would open one eye to look at me occasionally. I began to trust him and I quietly walked to him and petted him. As I reached to him, he stood up. I became a small child and we romped and played together. I trusted him as an innocent child!

Several small children joined us and the lion took us for a journey up the most beautiful mountain trail I have ever seen; and dangerous, too. We were not afraid because we felt loved, protected, joyous and free. And we didn't need to know where we were going!

I understood with more clarity that this ego self we have made makes us feel separated from the will of God. When we feel separated from God's will, we are fearful, feel unsafe, limited and unloved, and we become fearful of ourselves — our self-made self. To protect the self we have made we deny our fear and project our fear onto God and perceive him as a punishing God. When my fears were released, I was free to trust God and perceive him as a loving God. Also, I learned my higher Self and God's will are the same and my freedom, peace and joy come from trusting that Self.

In the last scene, I looked up into the sky to see the outline of the head of a gigantic lion, the symbol of God. That lion's head descended slowly to Earth and transformed itself into everything on Earth — the people, animals, plants, water, air, and soil. At that moment, I experienced the oneness of all creation, and understood that in reality we are not separate from each other or our Source.

FORGIVENESS

EXCERPTS FROM RELATED SOURCES

As prayer is always for yourself, so is forgiveness always given you. It is impossible to forgive another, for it is only your sins you see in him. You want to see them there, and not in you. That is why forgiveness of another is an illusion. Yet it is the only happy dream in all the world; the one that does not lead to death. Only in someone else can you forgive yourself, for you have called him guilty of your sins, and in him must your innocence now be found. Who but the sinful need to be forgiven? And do not ever think you can see sin in anyone except yourself.

Song of Prayer, page 10.

Your brother's errors are not of him, any more than yours are of you. Accept his errors as real, and you have attached yourself. If you would find your way and keep it, see only truth beside you for you walk together. The Holy Spirit in you forgives all things in you and in your brother. His errors are forgiven with yours. Atonement is no more separate than love. Atonement cannot be separate because it comes from love.

A Course in Miracles, Text, page 156.

Forgiveness is the key to happiness. I will awaken from the dream that I Am mortal, fallible and full of sin, And know I am the perfect Son of God.

A Course in Miracles, Workbook, page 212.

Follow the Holy Spirit's teaching in forgiveness, then, because forgiveness is His function and He knows how to fulfill it perfectly. That is what I meant when I said that miracles are natural, and when they do not occur, something has gone wrong. Miracles are merely the sign of your willingness to follow the Holy Spirit's plan of salvation, recognizing that you do not understand what it is. His work is not your function, and unless you accept this, you cannot learn what your function is.

A Course in Miracles, Text, page 158.

Unless the past is over in my mind, the real world must escape my sight. For I am really looking nowhere; seeing but what is not there. How can I then perceive the world forgiveness offers? This the past was made to hide, for this the world that can be looked on only now. It has no past. For what can be forgiven but the past, and if it is forgiven it is gone.

A Course in Miracles, Workbook, page 432.

Session 8

Forgiveness Workshop
Continued

Session 8

FORGIVENESS WORKSHOP CONTINUED

I.   PURPOSE

1. Discuss the concept, "This instant is the only time there is," from *Love Is Letting Go of Fear*.

2. Experience forgiveness through a written exercise and visualization.

II.   PROCEDURE

1. Visualization and meditation

Guide the following meditation and visualization:

Take three deep breaths to relax your minds and bodies. Visualize a light at the heart center of each of our bodies. Watch that light grow to cover each of our bodies and form a circle of light. A bright light from the Universe which represents love now connects with our circle of light. In your imagination, you see a large open upturned hand which fills that circle of light. That hand symbolizes "the hand of God which takes away all fear". Into that hand, place all your fears, frustrations, anxieties and attack thoughts. (Time) May all minds be joined as one mind with the Christ Mind without limit to send love wherever it is needed in the world. (Time)

End with the "Prayer for Guidance." When you are ready, return your attention to the group.

2. Lesson

Read lesson 8, page 105, in *Love Is Letting Go of Fear*. "This Instant is the Only Time There Is." Invite each member to relate an experience from the week when this concept helped the person experience an event with less fear. Suggest that the members form smaller groups and practice facilitating.

The purpose of our training is twofold. We present the concepts and principles as a framework for intellectually understanding attitudinal healing, and we experience that healing as we accept and forgive one another. Since each of us is a reflection of the love and fear we feel for ourselves, we can learn to love and accept ourselves as we love and forgive each other. We learn again that to give is to receive. As we release our fears and guilt through forgiveness, we learn to experience and teach peace of mind.

It is humanly impossible to totally overlook or forgive because we are just learning. The most important concept to remember is to forgive yourself for not forgiving another person. We are practicing. Try to love yourself regardless of what you think or how you feel!

3. **Forgiveness exercise**

Give the members the forgiveness exercise included in the lesson. Explain that after they answer the questions on that sheet they will be guided in a forgiveness visualization. Ask them to choose a person toward whom they hold grievances and want to forgive so they will be happier.

When you are comfortable in your chairs, close your eyes and take several deep breaths to relax your mind and body. (Time) Imagine you are observing this scene as if it were a play:

Imagine yourself in your peaceful place — in a woods, by a stream, in the mountains or on a beach. Still yourself as you sit quietly and become more peaceful. (Time)

The play starts. You see the person you have written about coming toward you. Become aware of all the feelings you have about this person. The person is now standing in front of you. Take time to answer the following questions: How do you think the other person is feeling about you? (Time) What are your feelings about this person? (Time) What are your feelings about yourself? (Time)

You decide this time you will see them differently. Now ask yourself these questions and allow yourself to hear the answers. Is it possible that what I feel about this person is really what I feel about myself? (Time) Am I now willing to look past the grievances and self doubt knowing willingness is all I need and my higher self, God, will do the rest? (Time)

Now you see a light at the heart center of the person and it grows to cover their entire body. You also see a light grow from your heart center to cover your body, and the two lights connect as one light. That light, which is love, heals the unforgiveness of both of you. Now bring your attention back to your peaceful place and enjoy the peace. (Time) When you are ready, open your eyes and bring yourself back to the room.

After the visualization, invite the members to relate whatever they would like about their experience. Some will have new insights they may want to share.

4. Assignment

Assign lesson 9, page 111 of *Love Is Letting Go of Fear*, "The Past is Over It Can Touch Me Not," for the following session. Write the lesson on a card.

Read "Self-Esteem" article in Additional Resources, p. 92.

5. Closing

Close the meeting in a circle with a short statement such as, "We are grateful for this opportunity to teach each other to love and forgive."

FORGIVENESS EXERCISE SHEET

Choose a person toward whom you hold grievances, someone you want to forgive, so you can have more peace of mind.

Describe how you think this person feels about you.

Describe your feelings about him or her.

Describe how you feel about your unforgiveness of this person.

Session 9

Fears Experienced With Serious Illness

Session 9

FEARS EXPERIENCED WITH SERIOUS ILLNESS

I.   PURPOSE

1.   Learn the concept, "The Past is Over It Can Touch Me Not", from *Love Is Letting Go of Fear.*

2.   Discuss some of the fears experienced by children with serious illnesses and their family members.

3.   Discuss what attitudes can help the facilitator deal with his or her fears of illness and death.

4.   Discuss the common concerns of people when they start facilitating attitudinal healing.

II.   PROCEDURE

1.   Meditation and visualization

Open meeting with the following meditation and visualization:

Take three deep breaths to relax your mind and body. Imagine yourself on a huge sailboat. You are sitting in a reclining deck chair on the stern of the boat. The weather is warm and you can see the reflection of the sun in the late afternoon on the calm sea. The wind is moving you slowly and gently. Feel the peace. (Time) If you have fear thoughts you want to release, imagine them as pink clouds escaping your mind and dissipating into the atmosphere. Spend time just being at peace. (Time)

Now visualize all of us together sitting in a circle on the boat. See the love that surrounds us as a large circle of light. Let our minds unite as One with the Christ Mind without limit to send love to the world wherever it is needed.

End with the "Prayer for Guidance."

2. Lesson

Read lesson 9, page 111, "The Past is Over, It Can Touch Me Not," from *Love Is Letting Go of Fear*. Invite each member to relate an experience this week which has helped him to understand this lesson.

3. Fears experienced in families with an ill child

Summarize fears of the seriously ill child, his siblings and parents outlined in "Fears Experienced in Families with an Ill Child," included in this session.

4. Common fears of facilitators

Discuss the common questions and concerns people have about facilitating attitudinal healing in groups or individually. Also, explore ways of perceiving these concerns that can help us release our fears. These concerns are explained in "Common Fears of Facilitators" included in this session.

5. A gentle death

A summary of *A Gentle Death*, Elizabeth Callari, R.N.,included in this session, describes the attitudes which are helpful in "being with" a dying person as they make their transition from Earth.

6. Assignment

Assign lesson 10, page 117 of *Love Is Letting Go of Fear*, "I Could See Peace Instead of This," and ask the members to write it on a card.

7. Closing

Close the meeting in a circle with a final statement, a poem or a song.

III.   SUGGESTED READINGS

1. Callari, Elizabeth S., R.N. *A Gentle Death: Personal Caregiving To The Terminally Ill.*

2. Deford, Frank. *ALEX, The Life of a Child.*

FEARS EXPERIENCED IN FAMILIES WITH AN ILL CHILD

One of the most common worries of a sick child is that if death comes, the parents will be too sad to go on living a happy, productive life. As stated in *There Is a Rainbow Behind Every Dark Cloud*, a book written by the children at the Center for Attitudinal Healing in Tiburon, California, these children avoid upsetting their parents by learning not to ask certain questions about death, such as, "Why do I have to die?" or "What will happen to me when I die?," even though they desperately need to have their questions answered and to talk about their fears.

The children expressed their feelings this way. "After we were told what our sickness was and that we might die from it, we were mad that it happened to us. The 'not knowing' if we were going to get well really bothered us. Hearing that we were going to get lots of shots and lose our hair also scared us."

"We did not look forward to getting x-ray therapy and chemotherapy because lots of times it made us feel worse, even though we knew it was given to us to make us well."

"It was hard for most of us to talk about how we felt inside. And it was hard for us to find someone who would really listen without being afraid."

Children wonder, "Why me?" and may think their illness or treatment is punishment from God, the doctor, or their parents. They fear that all the special attention they get from their parents will make their siblings jealous, and they fear rejection of their siblings. They feel isolated, also, from their peers since they can't participate in the school and social activities as they did before their illness. They miss school, may get behind in their school work, and can't play as they did before. They may be embarrassed and fear ridicule because of their hair falling out, their wigs, bandages, or any other medical accessory they may have to wear.

Children do not want pity. A fifteen year old girl with cancer, at the Evanston Center, said, "I hate it when people are nice to me just because I'm sick. I want them to like me just because of who I really am."

Small children fear mutilation if they think they are going to die because they have seen animals mutilated in death.

The concerns of the well siblings are usually much different from those of their sick brother or sister. When parents have a sick child, they are often so consumed by their fears about that child, about caring for the child, that communication with other children in the family suffers. The well siblings often are not told exactly what is happening because the parents often cannot accept the reality of the seriousness of their child's illness. Also, they may be uncertain about the diagnosis for a considerable period of time. Meanwhile, all the siblings can see and feel is that their brother or sister is getting all the attention, and that makes them jealous and angry.

Siblings sense, however, that something very serious is going on and that their brother or sister might die. Also, they fear their own death. If their sibling could die then it is possible for them or their parents to die. Children, sometimes in anger, have wished their sick sibling would die, when the sibling becomes ill they fear their wish has caused the illness and possibly death. Siblings sometimes fear they will catch their sick sibling's disease.

The sibling is angry because he or she needs support and neither parent can help them because of their own fears. They feel abandoned by their sick sibling who does not play with them anymore. One child said, "I feel lonely not having a little brother to play with and beat up." Also, if they do hit their sick sibling, they are afraid the hit may cause them to die.

The sibling feels guilty about having fun when their sick sibling can't. They miss having a normal family — the fun they had together. They wonder, "why our family?" They are angry because their family is "different". They are embarrassed about physical changes in their sibling, ambulances coming, and all the changes brought about by illness.

Unlike the children, young adults are old enough to be concerned about whether or not they are receiving the correct medical treatment. They fear death.

Often their serious illness forces them, just as they are gaining their independence, to become dependent on their parents again. Their lives are put on hold: they often can't drive. Their schooling and careers are interrupted, and they no longer believe they are attractive to the opposite sex.

Their inability to live a normal life alienates them from their brothers and sisters. They feel they have been cheated of life as they watch their peers make it in the world. Some young people have to come to terms with the inability to have children.

They fear the resentment of their parents whose lives are controlled by the demands of their illness. They are afraid that their parents are disappointed in not having a productive child, from the world's point of view. These two factors make them feel guilty.

The concerns of the parents are many. They question their ability to find the right medical treatment. They worry about offending their doctor if they get a second opinion, and they are sometimes confused about differences in opinion as to the treatment procedure.

They fear the illness might have been caused by them because of improper diet, or stress, and they believe they might have lessened the stress in their home. They worry that the child, in his desire to protect them, will not tell them about serious physical symptoms. They fear the death of their child, and feel extreme alarm about any new symptoms of illness because they fear the disease may be worsening.

They worry that they are neglecting their other children. They often have irrational concern about a sibling's illness since they feel they could not cope with another sick child or the possible loss of another child. They are overly concerned that their sick child will have an accident because he is not as alert, and they wonder if they are destroying his feelings of adequacy by being overprotective.

They fear they will be rejected by their friends, and that their child will be rejected by his friends. Old friends sometimes cease to stay in touch because the child's illness reminds them of their own vulnerability to illness and death, and the loss of a loved one.

They mourn the loss of a healthy child, and ask "Why my child?" and they are often jealous of parents with healthy children. They worry about how to make each day the child has left as happy as possible, and feel guilty when they enjoy life when the child is not able to participate.

Often they are angry because they can't get on with their own life which has been interrupted by their child's illness; they have lost control of their own life as well as their child's. They are overwhelmed by the additional demands of time and energy made on them, and fear they cannot continue to cope with these demands: that makes them feel guilty. They fear prolonged illness will require full time care. They worry about the costs and appropriate facilities, and feel guilty when they think of not keeping the child at home.

Husbands and wives often feel isolated from each other. Each needs the support of the other and neither is able to give that support because of their fears about the sick child.

The Center becomes a place where family members can get the support from facilitators and other families they so desperately need. It is a place where their feelings of isolation and differentness can be overcome as they express their fears to others who really understand them. The participants feel free to talk about what they really fear, because they are accepted. Hopelessness can be changed to hope in the group members as they feel the support of the facilitators and staff who attempt to judge everyone as whole no matter what the age or circumstances. The Center can become a haven of social interaction and support for young adults.

Lisa, age fifteen, and her father, mother, eight year old brother and thirteen year old sister, came to our Center for support two months after Lisa had been diagnosed with ovarian cancer. Each of her family members attended their peer support groups for a year before she died. In the beginning, her father expressed his hopelessness because he had no control over his daughter's life or death, and his anger about being cheated by her illness as well as by the loss of both his parents who died of cancer the year before.

With the love and support of the other families and staff at the Center, her father gradually let go of his need to control, and his anger. He chose to be with Lisa in a way that both of them could find some happiness and meaning in their lives in her last days.

One evening in the parents' group, he said, "It's terrible what has happened to all of us. We have sick children who may leave us. We have no control over that. Now let's go to them before they leave and thank them for teaching us the most important thing in the world, and that is to love one another."

Fifty people from the Center went to her memorial service. The father wrote and read a beautiful tribute about her life, and his gratitude to her for being his daughter and teacher for that short time. When the Buddhist Priest pondered about the number of people at the service when he had been told that only the family would be there, her father said, "These people are all my family."

COMMON FEARS OF FACILITATORS

When we start facilitating attitudinal healing we have concerns about our ability to help, and to cope with crises. We will discuss some of these concerns and suggest ways of perceiving them so we will be freer of the fears accompanying them.

We wonder if we can help another person in the small amount of time we have with them. We need to trust there are others in a person's life who will be there for them, also. Only the time we give willingly and lovingly is helpful. Time given as a sacrifice is not helpful.

How can we be helpful to a group member if we haven't experienced and dealt with their specific fears? The other person becomes our teacher. We are dealing with the problem now, through our teacher. We are equal, and teachers to each other. We can trust that when we ask God guide us in what we say and do, we will know how to join to help each of us.

We may judge ourselves as failing when our group members do not appear less fearful after we have met together several times. We need to let go of all judgment of the results of our being with others. We can trust that if our intent is to love unconditionally, both of us have less fear. Ram Dass suggests, in his book, *How Can*

I Help, that we "be available to people but don't make them feel they have to use us." It is the joining without expectations or judgments that heals, that releases fear.

Attitudinal healing occurs when we can perceive others as whole in spite of their ill body or emotional distress. To visualize everyone as whole is to see through the eyes of love, not with physical eyes. When we visualize another person as whole, no matter what their age or condition, they feel whole, and they confirm our own wholeness. Then both our minds are healed.

We may believe we could not cope with the death of one of our group members. We need to understand death as a natural process. As birth is an opportunity to grow on Earth, death is a transition for growth as we leave Earth to another dimension of life. In reality there is no death. Often people who are dying sense it is time to leave and they have accepted death. So they become our teachers. Each time we are with someone who dies, we work through some unresolved personal issues around our own death. We grow to accept death and accept life. Joining with another person at death is a gift to us and to them.

Some people feel they are not prepared to facilitate an attitudinal healing group after they have completed the training. The hands-on experience of facilitating a group is the additional training we need to feel confident as a facilitator. The willingness to facilitate a group requires a leap of faith. We trust that we will be guided in what to say; we will learn to let go of the need to judge the outcome of our work and of ourselves; we will learn to function as an equal in the group; we trust that we can be the vehicle to channel the love which can help to heal the fears of the group members and ourselves.

A GENTLE DEATH
Elizabeth S. Callari, R.N.
Summary by Betty Spaulding

"Death can be ... a beautiful experience, being consciously aware of every moment," says Elizabeth Callari, R.N., writer of *A Gentle Death*, a book giving much practical guidance to those involved in helping the dying achieve a peaceful transition.

Shaped by her professional training ("In every nursing class, the spoken or unspoken watchword was: Don't become emotionally involved with your patients. Don't.") [page 10] Her work as a specialist in chemotherapy and counselling the terminally ill, and her own personal encounter with cancer, Callari has transformed her deep-rooted fear and dread of death into a positive and loving service to the dying.

The dying person needs most to retain control over his own dying process — to set the pace of treatment, to order his affairs, and to take charge of his own death. "When the dying person selects the tone, theme, and leading players in this last scene, a sense of closure is more likely to be achieved." (The dying person may choose to relinquish this role, but it is clearly his decision.) [page 33]

"Those facing death need the love and respect which affirm human worth and dignity. Caretakers in a variety of relationships with the dying can serve this fundamental need."

And, how does love express? [page 21] ... Callari shows, in *A Gentle Death*, that:

Love is sensitive to the creation of conditions that create distance. This may include certain habits of dress and behavior which accent the discrepancy between their life conditions—and diminish the status of the dying person. Labels limit and dehumanize.

Love is flexible to the needs of the moment. To serve others means putting aside one's own agenda in order to hear and respond. "I listen and laugh and cry ... or stay silent. I ... share my lunch or bring in a pizza. I run errands or carry messages." [page 19]

Love is "of the heart." Learning from books can, of course, be valuable, but "advanced levels of education and training emphasize analysis and logic, which is the last thing dying people need." [page 21] This kind of "listening" tends to be in the head ... which evaluates, categorizes, and labels according to scientific criteria.

Love recognizes the uniqueness of each person's death. Perhaps THE most difficult task is releasing preconceptions ... letting go of prejudices, judgmental attitudes and prior assumptions. "A caretaker cannot achieve the fullest potential in helping the dying without completing this task". [page 41] Unconditional love and unwavering respect must underlie every effort.

Love respects the wishes, needs, and desires of the dying person even when this involves great restraint "...the caregiver can, in a determination to do the most possible good, inadvertently let his or her own idea of what is good for the dying person dominate the strategy". [page 59]

> The care of the Jury's (Gramps) — where the family honored his withdrawal from food and drink — is in sharp contrast to the woman who was obsessed with feeding her husband, even over his protests. [page 59]

Love is mutual. "When we serve the needs of the dying, we better understand our own mortality and finite existence." Wisdom and understanding about death IS wisdom and understanding about life. Love and care given to others IS love and care to ourselves. The Golden Rule is more than a commandment, it is a FACT. Giving IS receiving. "Love is our only reason for possessing life. The love given by caregivers to the dying is returned ten-fold." [page 27]

Love shares. Families that express and share their love for each other — and for the dying person — are families which "...are able to accept the transition of death, let go of what was, and go forward with life as an everchanging experience." [page 30] Caregivers can often facilitate the sharing of feelings between family members in a non-threatening way, and "can also encourage more open communication and mutual respect among the dying and medical personnel." [page 35]

Love listens to the whole person. The dying do express their deepest needs.

Reflections of a patient (excerpts) [pages 38-39]

Inside my body is a person —

...listen to me
...feel with me
...preserve my now-fragile dignity ...enable me to keep my self-respect
...look at me when you speak to me
...give me tender loving care
...call me by name
...tell me who you are
...touch me ...tell me what you are going to do
...show me your compassion
...show me through your care that I am a person
...think not only of my body but my spirit
...offer me spiritual care
...pray with me — or for me
...cry with me
...help me to be strong
...respect me
...don't isolate me with rituals

Over and over Callari stresses the need for becoming truly involved in sharing, caring and learning. While her background and psychology impelled her to seek answers, Callari's is a "hands on" experience of learning about dying from those inside that condition. What she shares in her book is her testimony to the joy and enrichment that comes from working with others for the benefit of the most frail among them. By working with and for the dying, we...

...learn a good deal about ourselves and others

...recognize in death something common to all
...confront our fears, our preconceptions, our prejudices
...enlarge our capacity for experiences of greater depth
...examine death and achieve a sense of comfort in its presence
...feel the reality of giving and receiving love

> "a love which evolves not from convenient, pleasant circumstances, but one which springs unhindered from the deepest human spirit." [page 121]

...achieve new hope.

> "Rather than experiencing despair at the inevitability of physical death, we can be up-lifted by the hope of an easy conscious death." [page 121]

> "Unlimited love ...
> means
> unlimited fullness of life.

Loving unconditionally
        completely
                without strings
                        is the purest form of love

Through our love of others,
        we grow
                teach
                        learn
                                become whole." [page 114]

Callari, Elizabeth. *A Gentle Death: Personal Caregiving to the Terminally Ill.* Copyright 1986. Available from: Tudor Publishers, Inc., P.O. Box 3443, Greensboro, NC 27402

Session 10

Releasing Blocks to Love

Session 10

RELEASING BLOCKS TO LOVE

I.   PURPOSE

1. Learn the concept, "I Could See Peace Instead of This," lesson 10, *Love is Letting Go of Fear*.

2. Discuss the process of becoming aware of love as fears are released.

3. Release blocks to love with a writing, meditation and visualization exercise.

II.   PROCEDURE

1. Visualization and meditation

Open the meeting with the following visualization and meditation. This meditation will be short because a meditation will be a part of the releasing blocks to love process.

As I name the part of your body, visualize light in that part and feel it relax you. Toes, ankles, calves, knees, thighs, lower torso, stomach, heart, lungs, fingers, arms, throat, tongue, nose, eyes, brain, and the top of your head.

Now transfer yourself to your most peaceful place and be quiet there and feel the peace. If thoughts come to your mind, let them ascend as pink clouds. (Time)

Now return your attention to this room and let our minds be joined as One and joined with the One Mind to send love to the world wherever it is needed.

End with the "Prayer for Guidance."

2. Lesson

Read lesson 10, page 117 in *Love is Letting Go of Fear*, "I Could See Peace Instead of This." Invite each member to relate an experience in which they felt less conflict because they remembered this concept.

3. Releasing blocks to love

Discuss "Releasing Blocks to Love" included in this session, which describes the fear of change as we release fear, and the joy in becoming more aware of love, as we let go of fear - the past.

4. Releasing blocks to love exercise

Give the members sheets of paper and pencils. Guide them in writing the releases as described in the sheet, "Steps In Releasing to Love Process," included in this session.

After the exercise, invite people to describe their experience with this exercise.

5. Assignment

Assign lesson 11, "I Can Elect to Change All Thoughts that Hurt" in *Love is Letting Go of Fear*, page 123.

6. Closing

Ask one of the members to close the meeting in a circle.

III. BACKGROUND INFORMATION FOR TRAINER

Excerpts from *A Course in Miracles, Text*, pages 203, 204, 205 (included in this session)

RELEASING BLOCKS TO LOVE

To release our fears is the most important process for understanding ourselves, and experiencing our true nature - that loving, lovable self. We need to know that although the rewards of letting go of our fears are great, we may at times experience feelings of loss of self. We may doubt our choice to become aware of our natural peaceful and loving nature. I will describe four dreams which deepened my understanding of the process of awakening to our true nature.

Since 1981, I have used a releasing-blocks-to- love process which Marilyn Anderson taught me. At that time, I was tired and filled with conflict because I was afraid to let go of what I perceived as my role as a mother and wife. I felt guilty when

I didn't function in both these roles as I had in the past when my three children were young. I continued to add activities and experiences to my life yet I would not release any of my past roles.

I asked to be released of my past perceptions of my role as mother and wife so I would be free to live in the present and have greater inner peace. After the release, a mediation imagery corrected those perceptions. I looked into the sky where I saw a 50-foot tall man constructed of large geometric pieces of glass, the colors of the rainbow. He stood before me shining magnificently in the sun, and dancing. He represented the wholeness and joy of my husband, each of my children, and of myself. I knew that if I could see each of my family members and myself as contemporary and eternally joyous, whole people, I could let go of my old belief that I had to take care of them as I had in the past. I could release the guilt I felt so I would be truly freer to live in the moment and love. On another level, that image symbolized the wholeness of each person on Earth, and helped me remember that eternally every individual is whole and perfect.

I found that sometimes I was not willing to release my old ways of perceiving. I was afraid of the unknown. The familiar seemed safer to me even if it was fearful. I was accustomed to that fear and guilt.

An image helped me understand that fear. A large old oak tree was growing at the top edge of a steep sheer mountain. Some of the roots were extended out over a deep, dark, wide crevice between two mountains. I saw myself hanging on to one of those roots, unable to climb back onto the mountain and afraid to let go. That mountain represented my past which I was releasing. I was afraid to let go completely because I would drop into what looked like a bottomless pit.

I was afraid to experience the unknown. It seemed dark and fearful and I felt I would destroy myself.

Three months later, the image reoccurred. In this image, I let go of the root of the old oak tree and I felt myself falling, falling and falling through the darkness as if there were no bottom. Finally, I saw a light beneath me. I felt my feet touch a surface. As I looked around a bright light revealed to me the most beautiful environment I have ever seen, and I felt total peace. You might say it seemed like heaven on Earth. I had let go of the fear of change, the fear of letting go of old perceptions so I could be freer to experience life in a new way — more fully and with trust and greater peace.

Recently, an image showed me we can let go of past fears and see only love — the light in the past. I was shown my childhood home in the country in central Illinois. A huge hackberry tree, about six feet in radius, still grows in the yard. It held a wooden porch swing when I was a child, and was near our windmill. On a high limb of this tree was a dark cocoon which enveloped a grown person. The cocoon opened and a person dropped to the ground. It was I who dropped out of that cocoon onto the ground. Doves and lambs, symbols of peace, joined me. As I looked toward our old home, I saw a bright light, love, shining in the middle of the house and it grew to fill the entire house.

I walked into the dining room where my mother sat doing needlework and rocking in a chair. Sun shone in the window through a lace tablecloth which covered our dining table. Peace surrounded me as it had as a child when I saw this scene. When I looked again, my mother appeared as a stuffed doll. The physical life of my mother was gone — only the eternal love remained.

In the last scene, I was standing in the yard and I saw the house fall in a heap of lumber to the ground and disappear, and the only thing remaining was the bright light. The only part left of the past was the love. This dream became a model to me of what is possible when we release the past. The physical impermanent manifestations of life no longer dominate my memory as reality. Only the love remained, and still remains in my mind.

The commitment to let go of our socialized, habitual, fearful, but familiar way of being in the world so we can reperceive the world and ourselves more peacefully, requires patience and trust.

STEPS IN RELEASING TO LOVE PROCESS

1. Ask each participant to choose a fear they are willing, this instant, to release, in writing, and also something they feel comfortable talking about in the group.

2. Suggest that each member listen carefully to all the other members' releases, and write those releases for themselves that they, too, would like to release.

3. As the training facilitator, ask that you be guided in helping each person express the fear they are trying to describe. Sometimes the facilitator can reword a release to clarify it. Always ask the participant if the restated release sounds right. Remember it is their release!

4. Ask the group members to close their eyes and be silent and ask that what they need to release be clarified for them.

5. Start writing the release this way: "I do now willingly release to a higher power (Universal Mind, Jesus, God, Buddha, my Higher Self, Love, whatever terms each individual calls the Higher Power) for correction ..."

6. Continue the release with one of the following phrases: "My misperception that; fear that; obstacles to; memory of; expectation that; unforgiveness of; need for revenge; investment in; attachment to; resistance to; anger toward; or disappointment in."

7. Example: RELEASE - "I do now willingly release to the Higher Power my misperception that Jean is rejecting me."

8. In writing the replacement, ask that the fear be replaced with such phrases as: "trust in my Higher Self; feelings of worthiness; greater inner peace and joy; forgiveness; happiness."

9. Example: REPLACEMENT - "I now accept feelings of worthiness and greater peace of mind."

10. Ask the participants to close their eyes and image, as in a play, that they are on a patio with an entity which represents that "Higher Power" to whom we have written our releases. Visualize giving the paper on which the releases are written to that loving entity who can "take away all fears." Say "thank you," meditate, and do not allow your mind to think about the release. Let thoughts become clouds and dissipate in the atmosphere. Meditate together for about five minutes.

RELEASING BLOCKS TO LOVE

Excerpts from *A Course in Miracles*

Little child, you are hiding your head under the cover of the heavy blankets you have laid upon yourself. You are hiding your nightmares in the darkness of your own false certainty, and refusing to open your eyes and look at them. (*Text*, page 203).

Let us not save nightmares, for they are not fitting offerings for Christ, and so they are not fit gifts for you. Take off the covers and look at what you are afraid of. Only the anticipation will frighten you, for the reality of nothingness cannot be frightening. Let us not delay this, for your dream of hatred will not leave you without help, and Help is here. Learn to be quiet in the midst of turmoil, for quietness is the end of strife and this is the journey to peace.

You cannot lay aside the obstacles to real vision without looking upon them, for to lay aside means to judge against. If you will look, the Holy Spirit will judge truly. Yet he cannot shine away what you keep hidden, for you have not offered it to Him and He cannot take it from you. (*Text*, page 204).

Whatever is given Him that is not of God is gone. Yet you must look at it yourself in perfect willingness, for otherwise His knowledge remains useless to you. Surely He will not fail to help you, since help is His only purpose. Do you not have greater reason for fearing the world as you perceive it, than for looking at the cause of fear and letting it go forever? (*Text*, page 205).

Session 11

Transition

Session 11

TRANSITION

I.   PURPOSE

1. Discuss how the concept, "I Can Elect to Change All Thoughts that Hurt," has affected our feelings this week.

2. Discuss the conflict and the resolution of feelings that result from new perceptions about self and relationships.

3. Express the experience and/or concept in the training which facilitated the greatest self-understanding and freedom from fear.

II.   PROCEDURE

1. Visualization and meditation

Open meeting with the following visualization and meditation:

Transport yourself to a warm sunny beach where you have felt the most peaceful. See everyone here with you in a circle sitting on that beach, and feel the warmth of the sun on your body. Feel the healing light of the sun penetrate each cell of your body, and imagine it lighting up each cell. All of our bodies make a circle of light — a lighted circle which heals all fears. Take time to feel the peace and release any fear or unforgiveness. (Time)

Return your attention to this room and let our minds join with the One Mind to be channels to send love to the world wherever it is needed. (Time)

End with the "Prayer for Guidance."

When you are ready, return your attention to the room.

2. Lesson

Read lesson 11, "I Can Elect to Change All Thoughts that Hurt" and discuss experiences which have been lightened by remembering the concept.

3. **"Transition" issues**

Read and discuss "Transition," included in this session. Encourage members to describe their experiences.

4. **Group discussion of training program**

Invite the participants to describe the experiences in the training which have been most helpful and to suggest ways the training could be improved.

5. **Symptoms of inner peace**

Read and discuss "Symptoms of Inner Peace," included in this issue.

6. **Certificates of Participation**

Plan to present Certificates of Participation as a part of the final meeting's program.

7. **Assignment**

Assign lesson 12, page 128, "I Am Responsible for What I See" from *Love Is Letting Go of Fear*, for the next week.

8. **Closing**

Close the meeting in a circle.

III.   BACKGROUND INFORMATION FOR TRAINER

1. Excerpts from *A Course in Miracles, Text*, pages 156, 224, 506, 518; *Manual for Teachers*, page 8. (included in this session)

TRANSITION

When we begin to feel freedom from judgment, and peace, often we feel compelled to insist that our spouse, best friends and family members embrace our new beliefs. We need to remember we are not here to change people; our peace comes from accepting them and loving them. To be loving is to accept unconditionally all people's beliefs — to accept their paths as correct for them. Our most challenging lesson in forgiveness is to accept the path of the person closest to us when it is different from ours.

Our relationships with some of our friends can change. When our responses to them are more peaceful, when we do not support fear as we have in the past, our friends may believe we are not "realistic about the real world," and they may withdraw from us. This can come at a time when we feel "alone" with our new beliefs and unsure of them, and we need our friends to accept them so they are more valid to us. We need not feel rejected and doubtful. Love is eternal and never lost, and is not dependent on time.

In the transition from the old familiar way of perceiving the world to the new more peaceful way, we live in both belief systems until we let go of the old and trust the new. During this time, we can feel a loss of identity and disorientation. We may also be faced with trials which we do not understand, which add to our feelings of confusion, discouragement and doubt. An image in meditation helped me to trust that all experiences have the purpose to teach us peace and trust.

I was in a rowboat in the middle of the ocean. I struggled to be "in control" of the boat as I maneuvered it with two oars. As I fearfully decided to "let go of control," I dropped the oars. My fears were symbolized by four whales which appeared and frolicked around the boat making big waves which rocked it furiously. And I felt so alone. The whales and ocean waves represented the terror we feel when we let go of the familiar, and I felt the "aloneness" which characterizes our feeling as we leave the familiar. Suddenly, the four whales, one on each corner of the boat, steadied the boat with their noses and the ocean calmed.

As the whales quieted the boat, I learned to trust them, and that trust was reinforced as the boat was transformed into a wooden platform. As I sunbathed in peace, the ocean became even calmer and railings appeared on the platform which made me feel more protected. An angel- like being descended onto the platform, and I became that being; a symbol of the reality of all of us — the eternal self without fear.

When we let go of our fears, the danger we feel from letting go as represented by the whales, is transformed into a blessing— safety and peace. Each step of the way we learn to trust because our experience teaches us it is not only safe to trust but that we are being guided on an adventurous, joyous, peaceful journey.

SYMPTOMS OF INNER PEACE

1.   A tendency to think and act spontaneously rather than on fears based on past experiences.

2.   An unmistakable ability to enjoy each moment.

3.   A loss of interest in judging other people.

Our values cannot be determined by our thoughts, behavior or accomplishments; our value is already established by God.

When we commit ourselves to experiencing life in a more harmonious and peaceful way, we can trust we will have many experiences in life to teach us to return to our loving, innocent, trusting and peaceful childlikeness. Some of the lessons are joyous and others difficult. In the beginning, the discomfort and guilt can be viewed with fear. As we learn to trust that all experiences have the purpose to teach, we can accept the difficult ones as a way to lead us to correction; and we will embrace them and accept them as blessings. Since all experiences are for growth, they cannot be judged as "good" or "bad"; they are neutral.

All lessons are to teach us to let go of our judgment of others, ourselves and the world. When we choose to let go of our judgments and grievances, we are free to love and be guided by our intuition, our inner guidance, which directs us to live peacefully with one another. Trusting our inner guidance will allow us to let go of the attachment to the results of our efforts and trust that the outcome is always correct for learning. People experience our love and their wholeness when we trust their unique process for growth. We acknowledge we cannot judge them by their past or our limited ego evaluation.

Our socialized habit of evaluating, analyzing and judging makes us unhappy. We can change that habit by a continuous effort to release that socialized pattern of thinking to our higher self for correction.

We are not victims of the world we see. We always project onto the world the thoughts, feelings and attitudes which preoccupy us. We can choose to see the world differently by releasing our grievances and replacing our fear thoughts with love.

We strive not to judge the present or future by the past so we are freer to live in the present; we are free of the past when we forgive.

We are all equal and we are both teachers and students to one another.

Love is the greatest healing force in the world. The law of love teaches that to love another person means to listen without judgment and to see the eternal wholeness of the other person no matter what the circumstances.

The law of love requires we ask for help to release fears and forgive; that we trust God, the Universe, our Higher Self.

Unloving responses are a call for love rather than a personal attack.

4.   A loss of interest in interpreting the actions of others.

5.   A loss of interest in conflict.

6.   A loss of the ability to worry.

7.   Frequent overwhelming episodes of appreciation.

8.   Contented feelings of connectedness with others and with nature.

9.   Frequent attacks of smiling.

10.   An increased tendency to let things happen rather than to make them happen.

11.   An increased susceptibility to the love extended by others as well as an uncontrollable urge to extend it.

Saskia Davis

TRANSITION

Excerpts from *A Course in Miracles.*

To use the power God has given you as He would have it used is natural. It is not arrogant to be as He created you, nor to make use of what He gave to answer all his Son's mistakes and set him free. But it is arrogant to lay aside the power that He gave, and choose a little senseless wish instead of what He wills. The gift of God to you is limitless. There is no circumstance it cannot answer, and no problem which is not resolved within its gracious light. (*Text*, page 518).

It is not difficult to understand the reasons why you do not ask the Holy Spirit to solve all problems for you. He has not greater difficulty in resolving some than others. Every problem is the same to Him, because each one is solved in just the same respect and through the same approach. The aspects that need solving do not change, whatever form the problem seems to take. A problem can appear in many forms, and it will do so while the problem lasts. It serves no purpose to attempt to solve it in a special form. It will recur and recur again and yet again, until it has been answered for all time and will not rise again in any form. And only then are you released from it. (*Text*, page 506).

The teachers of God have trust in the world, because they have learned it is not governed by the laws the world made up. It is governed by a Power That is in them but not of them. It is this Power That keeps all things safe. It is through this Power that the teachers of God look on a forgiven world. (*Manual for Teachers*, page 8).

When a brother behaves insanely, you can heal him only by perceiving the sanity in him. If you perceive his errors and accept them, you are accepting yours. If you want to give yours over to the Holy Spirit, you must do this with his. Unless this becomes the one way in which you handle all errors, you cannot understand how all errors are undone. How is this different from telling you that what you teach you learn? Your brother is as right as you are, and if you think he is wrong, you are condemning yourself. (*Text*, page 156).

This course has explicitly stated that its goal for you is happiness and peace. Yet you are afraid of it. You have been told again and again that it will set you free, yet you sometimes react as if it is trying to imprison you. You often dismiss it more readily than you dismiss the ego's thought system. To some extent, then, you must believe that by not learning the course you are protecting yourself. And you do not realize that it is only your guiltlessness that can protect you.

The Atonement has always been interpreted as the release from guilt, and this is correct if it is understood. Yet even when I interpret it for you, you may reject it and do not accept it for yourself. You have perhaps recognized the futility of the ego and its offerings, but though you do not want them, you may not yet look upon the alternative with gladness. (*Text*, page 224).

Session 12

Summary

Session 12

SUMMARY

I.   PURPOSE

1. Discuss how the concept, "I Am Responsible for What I See," has helped change your perception.

2. Review attitudinal healing concepts and discuss how they can be used as a way of living in all relationships.

3. Encourage members to express their present and future interests as participants in the Center's programs (if applicable), and invite program suggestions.

4. Present Certificates of Participation.

II.   PROCEDURE

1. Visualization and meditation

Guide the following visualization and meditation:

Take several deep breaths and relax your mind and body. Visualize yourself as the innocent trusting child which still exists within each of us. Quiet yourself and allow a picture of yourself to return to when you were that free, happy child. (Time) Observe that child. (Time) See what they are doing. (Time) Let yourself experience what they are feeling. Ask questions about any conflicts you have and listen to the child's answer. Remember the child lives fully in the moment, they forgive, they trust and they have few fears. Become that child for awhile. (Time) When you are ready, become a member of our group in this room and let our minds be joined with the One Mind to channel love to wherever it is needed.

End with the "Prayer for Guidance."

2. Lesson

Read lesson 12, "I Am Responsible for What I See" and describe experiences which have helped you understand this concept.

3. **Review of attitudinal healing concepts**

   Discuss attitudinal healing concepts as described in "Review of Attitudinal Healing Concepts," included in this session.

   Invite the participants to describe how the attitudinal healing concepts are useful in their present personal and work lives.

4. **Discussion**

   Encourage each person to express their interest in participating in further programs at the Center (if applicable). Trainees are a source for evaluating community needs for groups, evaluating the present training program, and suggesting additional educational programs.

5. **Present certificates**

   Certificates of recognition of participation in the training program can be presented.

6. **Closing**

   Close the meeting in a circle and ask people who would like to make a closing statement to participate.

III. BACKGROUND INFORMATION FOR FACILITATOR TRAINER

1. *A Course in Miracles, Text*, page 404 (Resource section)

2. "Miracles Still Happen," Robert Redd (Resource section)

3. Reread "Jeremy," (Resource section)

REVIEW OF ATTITUDINAL HEALING CONCEPTS

Attitudinal healing is replacing fear with love so we can experience more joy and inner peace. When we exchange our physical eyes for the eyes of love, we see the level of the laws of love, and we can see with the vision of love. Our physical senses can discern only a fragment of our true self. In eternity we are whole, perfect children of God. Through the eyes of love we can learn to believe in the eternal wholeness of everyone.

We are like antennae extending love wherever it is needed as our fears are released. When we extend love as through meditation, prayer and our presence, we feel our connectedness with all others, and learn that giving love is receiving love.

The law of love is that we are love so as we give love to others, we teach ourselves what we are.

Problems can be solved peacefully when they are released to the higher power and we ask that our intuition guide us in our participation in their resolutions. That is why these concepts are applicable to all situations.

Since these concepts are goals, we need to be constantly releasing our judgment of ourselves as inadequate as we practice them. Our most important function is to accept and love ourselves just as we are. We are love at this moment! We are learning to be aware of it!

I wish you a joyous journey!

Resources

RESOURCES

The following story is taken from *PARABOLA, The Magazine of Myth and Tradition*, Volume XI, NUMBER 2, MAY, 1986, published by the Society for the Study of Myth and Tradition, Inc., and distributed by Eastern News, 1130 Cleveland Road, Sandusky, Ohio 44870.

JEREMY

Jacques Lusseryan

Translated by Noelle Oxenhandler

The first man on my path is an old man. And you cannot imagine how happy this makes me.

I do not know if there is a greater blessing than to encounter a true old person, that is, one who is joyous. It is a blessing which is rarely given to us, because for most, alas, age is nothing but the blank and degrading addition of physical years. But when an old person is joyful, he is so strong that he no longer needs to speak; he comes and he heals. The one who fills my memory is like this. His name is Jeremy Regard.

It is not I who give him his name. It was his. How many novelists would like to have intended it?

I would like to be very modest, you know, in describing him, because he was so great and yet seemed it so little. He made such a brief passage through my life — only a few weeks — that I can no longer remember his body. I vaguely perceive a man who is vigorous, straight, thickset. Yes, a small man, according to physical measurements. As for his face, I can't see it. I think that I never asked myself any questions about his face, even then. I saw another which was much more real.*

I met him in January 1944, in the midst of the war, in Germany, when I was in a concentration camp at age nineteen. He was one of the six thousand French who arrived in Buchenwald between the 22nd and 26th of January. But he was unlike any other.

Here I must stop for a moment, because I have written the word "Buchenwald." I will often be writing of it. But do not expect a picture of the horrors of the deportation. These horrors were real, and they are not pleasant to talk about. To have the right to speak about them, it would be necessary to be a healer — and not just of the body. I will content myself then with the indispensable, the basic scenario.

Sometimes I will even speak of the deportation in a manner which is scandalous for some, I mean paradoxical: I will say in what it was good, I will show what riches it contained.

If I came back to it sometimes, it is because it stands at the very entrance of my life, an attic bursting with pains and joys, with questions and answers.

Jeremy did not speak of the concentration camps either, even when he was there. He did not have his gaze nailed to the smoke from the crematorium, nor on the twelve hundred terrified prisoners of Block 57. He was looking through.

At first I didn't know who he was — people spoke to me of "Socrates."

My neighbors, who were very numerous, pronounced this name which was utterly unexpected in the swarming fear and cold in which we tossed. "Socrates said...," "Socrates laughs..." Socrates was over there, a little further, on the other side of this crowd of closely shaven men. I did not understand why all these people called one person out of everyone Socrates. But I wished to meet him.

Finally one day I saw him — that is, I must have seen him, for to tell the truth, I have no memory of the first meeting.

I know only that I was expecting an eloquent reasoner, a clever metaphysician, some sort of triumphant moral philosopher. That is not at all what I found.

He was a simple welder from a small village at the foot of the Jura mountains. He had come to Buchenwald for reasons which had so little to do with the essential that I never knew them or asked about them.

His name was not Socrates, as you already know, but Jeremy, and I didn't understand why this name wasn't enough for his companions.

Jeremy's tale was that of a welder from a particular part of the world, a village in France. He loved to tell it with broad smiles. He told it very simply, as any tradesman talks about his trade. And here and there one could just barely glimpse a second forge standing there, a forge of the spirit.

Yes, I said "spiritual". However, the word has been spoiled by overuse. But this time it is true and full.

I heard Jeremy speak of men who did not come to his shop just for their horses and their wagons but for themselves. They came so as to go home all steeled and new, to take home a little of the life they were lacking and which they found overflowing, shining and gentle at the forge of father Jeremy.

At this time I was a student. I had hardly ever experienced such men, they do not fill the universities. I thought that when a man possessed wisdom, he immediately said it, and said how and why according to which affiliation of thought. Especially, I thought that in order to be wise, it was necessary to think, and to think rigorously.

I stood with my mouth open before Jeremy because he didn't think. He told stories, almost always the same, he shook your shoulders, he seemed to be addressing invisible beings through you. He always had his nose smack in the obvious, close- at- hand. If he spoke about the happiness of a neighbor upon leaving his shop, it was as if he spoke about a wart, a bump, which had just been removed. He observed things of the spirit with his eyes, as doctors observe microbes through their microscopes. He made no distinction. And the more I saw him do this, the more the weight of the air diminished for me.

I have encountered startling beings, beings whose gestures and words so dazzled that in their presence one had to lower one's eyes. Jeremy was not startling. Not a bit! He wasn't there to stir us up.

It was not curiosity which impelled me toward him. I needed him as a man who is dying of thirst needs water. Like all important things, this was elemental.

I see Jeremy walking through our barracks. A space formed itself among us. He stopped somewhere and, all at once, men pressed in tighter, yet still leaving him a little place in their midst. This was a completely instinctive movement which one cannot explain simply by respect. We drew back rather as one steps back to leave a place for one who is working.

You must picture that we were more than a thousand men in this barracks, a thousand where four hundred would have been uncomfortable. Imagine that we were all afraid, profoundly and immediately. Do not think of us as individuals, but as a protoplasmic mass. In fact, we were glued to one another. The only movements we made were pushing, clutching, pulling apart, twisting. Now you will better understand the marvel (so as not to say "miracle") of this small distance, this circle of space with which Jeremy remained surrounded.

He was not frightening, he was not austere, he was not even eloquent. But he was there, and that was tangible. You felt it as you feel a hand on the shoulder, a hand which summons, which brings you back to yourself when you were about to disappear.

Each time he appeared, the air became breathable: I got a breath of life smack in the face. This was perhaps not a miracle, but it was at least a very great act, and one which he alone was capable. Jeremy's walk across the quad was that: a breathing. In my memory I can follow distinctly the path of light and clarity which he made through the crowd.

I didn't understand then who he was, but certainly I saw him. And this image began to work inside me until the moment it lit up like a torch. I didn't know who he was because he didn't say.

He had a story which he came back to often: it belonged, he belonged, to the Christian Science sect. He had even been to America once to meet his fellow Christian Scientists. This adventure, quite out of the ordinary for a welder from the Jura, intrigued but did not enlighten me. It gave another layer of mystery to his character. That was all. Jeremy, without stories, mattered.

Is it necessary to apologize for using so many images which are linked to simple acts: to eating, to breathing? If I were tempted to do so, Jeremy would prohibit me. He knew too well that one does not live on ideas.

He was a truly manual man. He knew that at Buchenwald we would not live on the ideas which we had of Buchenwald. He said this; he even said that many of us would die from them. Alas, he was not mistaken.

I knew there were men who died because people had killed them.

For them there was nothing left to do but to pray. But I also knew many who died very quickly, like flies, because they thought they were in hell. It was of such matters that Jeremy spoke.

It was necessary for there to be a man as simple, as clear, who had gone to the depths of reality, in order to see the fire and beyond the fire. More than hope was needed.

It was necessary to see.

The good man Jeremy saw. There was a spectacle before his eyes, but it was not the one we saw. It was not our Buchenwald, that of the victims. It was not a prison, that is to say, a place of hunger, blows, death, protect, where other men, the evil ones, had committed the crime of putting us. For him, there were not us, the innocents, and the other, the big anonymous Other with the tormenting voice and the whip - "The brute."

How did I know? You have the right to ask: After all, Jeremy said almost nothing about such things. Well, without a doubt, there exists in certain beings, as there existed in him, a rightness and wholeness so perfect that their way of seeing communicates itself, is given to you, for at least an instant.

And the silence then is truer, more exact, than any words.

When Jeremy came to us across Block 57, in the midst of his little halo of space, it was clarity which he gave to us. It was an overflowing vision, a new vision. And that is why we all made way for him.

Above all, do not imagine that Jeremy consoled us. At the point we had reached, any consolation would have been mere romance, a taunting nursery story. We were not in the land of Cockaigne, and if we had been crazy enough to think so for one second, waking up afterward would have been bitter indeed. Jeremy spoke hard. But he did so gently.

There was no trace of glibness about him. He had a mellow voice, precise and deliberate gestures, but this was the habit of his craft, a natural tranquility. He was a good fellow, I'm telling you, not a prophet.

Jeremy was so little a prophet, he created so little uproar, that I don't know how many, among the dozen men who survived those days of Winter 1944 in Barrack 57, remember him today. I would so much like not to be the only one.

One didn't notice anything special about Jeremy, no sign. He carried the banner of no faith, except from time to time that of Christian Science. But at this time, for me, and for the other Frenchmen around me, this word had only a bizarre resonance.

One went to Jeremy as toward a spring. One didn't ask oneself why. One didn't think about it. In this ocean of rage and suffering there was this island: a man who didn't shout, who asked no one for help, who was sufficient unto himself.

A man who did not dream: that was more important than anything. The rest of us were dreamers: we dreamed of women, of children, of houses, often of the very miseries of other times which we had the weakness to call "liberty". We weren't at Buchenwald. We didn't want anything to do with Buchenwald.

And each time we came back it was there just the same, and it hurt.

Jeremy was not disappointed. Why would he have dreamed? When we saw him coming with his immense serenity, we felt like shouting, "Close your eyes! What one sees here burns!" But the shout remained in our throats because, from all evidence, his eyes were solidly fixed on all our miseries and did not blink. Even more, he did not seem like someone who takes a great burden upon himself, the air of a hero. He was not afraid, and that just as naturally as we were afraid.

"For one who knows how to see, things are just as they always are," he said. At first I did not understand. I even felt something quite close to indignation. What? Buchenwald like ordinary life? Impossible. All of these crazed, hideous men, the howling menace of death, these enemies everywhere, among the S.S., among the prisoners themselves, this wedge of hill pushed up against the sky, thick with smoke, with its seven circles, and over there across the forest, the electric fences, all of this was just as usual! I remember that I could not accept this. It had to be worse — or if not — then more beautiful. Until finally Jeremy enabled me to see.

It was not a revelation, a flashing discovery of the truth. I don't think there was even an exchange of words. But one day it became obvious, palpable to me in the flesh, that Jeremy, the welder, had lent me his eyes.

With those eyes, I saw that Buchenwald was not unique, not even privileged to be one of the places of greatest human suffering. I also saw that our camp was not in Germany, as we thought, in the heart of the Thuringe, dominating the plain Iena, in this precise place and in no other. Jeremy taught me, with his eyes, that Buchenwald was in each one of us, baked and rebaked, tended incessantly, nurtured in a horrible way. And that consequently we could vanquish it, if we desired to with enough force.

"As always," Jeremy explained to himself sometimes. He had always seen people living in fear and in the most invincible of all fears: that which has no object. He had seen them all desire secretly and above all else one thing: to do harm to themselves. It was always, it was here, the same spectacle. Simply, the conditions had finally been completely fulfilled. The war, Nazism, the political and national follies had created a masterpiece, a perfect sickness and misery: a concentration camp.

For us, of course, this was the first time. Jeremy had no use for our surprise. He said that it was not honest and that it did us harm.

He said that in ordinary life, with good eyes, we would have seen the same horrors. We had managed to be happy before. Well! The Nazis had given us a terrible microscope: the camp.

This was not a reason to stop living.

Jeremy was an example: he found joy in the midst of Block 57. He found it during moments of the day where we found only fear. And he found it in such great abundance that when he was present we felt it rise in us. Inexplicable sensation, incredible even, there where we were: joy was going to fill us.

Imagine this gift which Jeremy gave us! We did not understand, but we thanked him, time and again.

What joy? Here are explanations, but they are feeble: the joy of being alive in this moment, in the next, each time we became aware of it. The joy of feeling the lives of others, of some others at least, against us, in the dark of night. What do I know? Isn't that enough for you?

It was much more than enough for us. It was a pardon, a reprieve, there, all of a sudden, just a few feet from hell. I knew this state through Jeremy. Others knew it also, I am sure.

The joy of discovering that joy exists, that it is in us, just exactly as life is, without conditions and which no condition, even the worst, can kill.

All of this, you will say, came from Jeremy because he was lucid. I didn't say that he was lucid — this quality belongs to intelligence and, in the world of intelligence, Jeremy was not at home. I said that he saw. I have spoken of him as a living prayer.

Subtle people will pretend that the faith of Jeremy was without nuances. Who cares! For him, and for us though him, the world was saved in each second. This benediction had no end. And, when it ceased, it was that we had ceased wanting it, that we — and not it — had ceased being joyful.

These are not great words. And if nonetheless you have that impression, then it is that I am clumsy. Ordinary and supernatural, that's it.

One could very well live next to him for weeks and not see him, and speak only of "an old guy not like the others." He was not a spectacle in the manner of heroes or street hawkers.

What was supernatural in him, from all evidence, didn't belong to him; it was meant to be shared. The spectacle, if it existed, was for us to find and to find within ourselves. I have the clearest memory of finding it. I perceived, one day like the others, a little place where I did not shiver, where I had no shame, where the death-dealers were only phantoms, where life no longer depended on the presence of the camp or on its absence. I owed it to Jeremy.

I have carried this man in my memories as one carries an image with one because it had been blessed.

And now, how has he disappeared? I hardly know. Without a sound, in any case, just as he came.

One day, someone told me that he had died. This must have been several weeks after our arrival in the camp.

Men went like this there. One almost never knew how. They disappeared in too great numbers all at once: nor one had either the time or the inclination to look into the details, the "how" of their death. We let them melt into the mass. There was a solid ground of death in which we all participated more or less, we who were alive. The death of others was so much our own affair that we didn't have the courage to look it in the face.

I do not know the "how" of Jeremy's departure. I remember only that he came to see me, several days earlier, and told me that it was the last time. Not at all in the way one announced an unhappy event, not so solemnly. Simply — this was the last time, and since it was thus he had come to tell me.

I don't think this caused me pain. It must not have been painful. Indeed it was not, because it was real and known.

He had been of service. He had the right to leave this world which he had completely lived.

I am well aware that people will say to me, "What do you see of the supernatural in your welder? He gave you an example of serenity, at a time when serenity was very difficult to attain. That's good, but that's all. This peace of Jeremy was the result of courage and a strong constitution."

Well, no! We will not have done with Jeremy for that price.

What I call the supernatural in him was the break with habits which he had completely realized. Those habits of judgment which make us call any adversity "unhappiness" or "evil," those of greed which make us hate, desire vengeance, or simply complain — a minor but incontestable form of hatred — those of our dizzying egocentricity which make us think that we are innocent each time we suffer. He had escaped from the network of compulsive reflexes, and it was this necessary movement which neither good health — or even perfect health, if such exists — can explain.

He had touched the very depth of himself and liberated the supernatural or, if this word bothers you, the essential, that which does not depend on any circumstance, which can exist in all places and in any time, in pain, as in pleasure. He had encountered the very source of life. If I have used the word "supernatural", it is because the act of

Jeremy sums up to me the religious act itself: the discovery that God is there, in each person, to the same degree, completely in each moment, and that a return can be made toward him.

This was the good news which Jeremy told, in his turn, and in his very humble manner.

We would all gain a lot by putting memory in quarantine. The petty memory, at least the stingy, encumbering memory which makes us believe in this unreality, this myth: the past.

It is this which suddenly brings back — without a shadow of reason — a person, or the shred of an event which then installs itself in us. The image throws itself on the screen of consciousness; it swells, soon there is nothing else but it. The mind's circulation stops. The present disperses. The moments which follow no longer have the force to carry us.

They no longer have any flavor. In short, this memory secretes melancholy, regret, all manner of inner complication.

Fortunately, there is the other memory. For me, it is the one to which Jeremy belongs.

This man haunts me, I confess. But he does not haunt me in the manner of a memory. Simply, he has entered into my flesh, he nourishes me, he works to make me live. I spend very little time thinking about him: one could say it is he who thinks of me.

To speak to you of him, I have had to allude to Buchenwald. But do not be misled: Jeremy was never "at Buchenwald." I encountered him there in flesh and blood. He wore a registration number. Others beside myself knew him. But he was not there in the particular, exclusive, individual manner in which we hear the phrase "to have been at Buchenwald."

This adventure of the camp was for him only an adventure: it did not concern him in a fundamental way.

There are people whom I remember only in letting the "little memory" function in me. These people, if I encountered them there, remain there. Jeremy, when he speaks to me, does not do so from out of my past, but from the depths of my present, there, right in the center. I cannot move him.

They are all this way, the people who have taught us something. Because this something, this knowledge, this increase of presence in life, they give to us only because they clearly know that they are not the owners. Imagine Jeremy happy as it happens to others to be happy: for personal reasons, due to history different from that of others, precious and subtle. Do you think that he would still be in my life?

He would have rejoined those picturesque characters, passing figures. But Jeremy was not happy: he was joyous. The good which he enjoyed was not his. Or rather, it was — but by participation. It was just as much ours.

This is the mystery and power of those beings who serve something other than their own provisional personalities: one cannot escape them.

Translated from *Le monde commence aujour-d' hui* by Jacques Lusseryan. [c] Editions de la Table Ronde, Paris, 1959. Used by permission.

*Jacques Lusseryan was blinded in a school accident at the age of eight. — Ed.

SELF ESTEEM

In 1984, The California Task Force to Promote Self- Esteem and Personal and Social Responsibility was formed. The enabling legislation was written by Assembly-man John Vasconcellos. He was responding to a personal struggle that he had experienced with developing his own self-esteem and also dealing with an extreme sense of frustration that came to him while working on the committee that sets forth the annual California budget. It had become apparent to Mr. Vasconcellos that a "social vaccine" was needed; it did no good to throw vast sums of money into help and welfare programs that responded too late to the social ills of contemporary society. So, a twenty- nine member panel of mental health professionals and educators was charged with making an in depth analysis of some of the major problems that large urban populations are facing. The areas that were studied are:

> School drop outs
> Delinquency/crime/incarceration
> Teenage pregnancy
> Drug and alcohol abuse
> Unemployment
> Illiteracy
> Homelessness

The Task Force's key finding was, "Self-esteem is the likeliest candidate for a social vaccine... The lack of self-esteem is central to most personal and social ills plaguing our state and nation as we approach the end of the twentieth century."*

Where has this chronic lack of self-esteem come from? Children are born as trusting and innocent little people with an innate sense of self-worth. The fears which cause low self-esteem are accumulated from birth as a result of many socialization experiences and misperceptions. Many of these fears are common to all of us, and include:

> Rejection - being laughed at, humiliated, ignored
> Abandonment
> Loss of love
> Not being understood
> Failure - at work, play, relationships
> Punishment
> Physical safety is threatened
> Hunger, cold
> Illness
> Death of a loved one

Fear of God
Fear of annihilation

The process of relearning our inherent value involves releasing the accumulated fears which are inhibiting the experience of knowing our true and lovable, well self.

The Task Force concluded that the primary ingredients of self-esteem are as follows:

A sense of belonging
Likability
A feeling of significance
Acknowledgement of hard work

To nurture self-esteem in ourselves and others, we need to become aware of and incorporate into our daily lives the following practices and ideals:

Accept ourselves and others
Forgive ourselves and others
Take risks/develop courage to face change
Set realistic goals
Trust ourselves and others
Express our feelings and respect the feelings of others
Appreciate our spiritual being
Appreciate our mind
Appreciate our body
Affirm each persons uniqueness
Give personal attention
Demonstrate respect, acceptance and support
Appreciate the benefits of a multi-racial culture
Negotiate rather than being abusive
Take responsibility for our own decisions and actions
Become a person of integrity

There are also levels of nurturing that can take place in the realm of social responsibility; how our social welfare systems can aid in building self- esteem. Attitudinal healing principles also guide us in this direction. In addition to the social ills that were listed previously, there are other levels of problems that many are familiar with: alienated relationships, not living life joyfully, and sometimes, even illness.

Attitudinal healing concepts go hand in hand with the "primary ingredients" of self-esteem as set forth by the Task Force. By learning the concepts and setting up an environment of small groups, attitudinal healing unblocks our innate self-esteem by releasing fear through:

Non-judgmental listening
Peer support in joining with others who understand
Releasing and expressing fear, guilt and unforgiveness by:
    sharing
    visualizations
    written expression
    art
    music
    discussion
    social activities
    discovering the "higher power", higher self, God
Celebrating the small and large successes of an adverse situation or just everyday life.

As we become more self-aware, our self-esteem grows. The results are myriad, but include, most importantly, an inner harmony which can permeate all of our interactions and inner-actions. We all learn to be unconditional in our acceptance of ourselves and others. We are lovable and important just because we exist.

* *Toward a State of Esteem.* California Task Force to Promote Self-Esteem and Personal and Social Responsibility, California State Department of Education, 1990, p. 4.

Parabola, Summer, 1988, Volume XIII, Number 2, May, 1988.

THE GOSPEL AS YOGA

Ravi Ravindra

The only reason that I, an outsider to the Christian tradition and not particularly learned in it, write about one of its most sacred texts is my love for it. The first time I encountered it, nearly a quarter of a century ago, I was much moved by The Gospel According to St. John. Since then I have read this Gospel many times; always it leaves me in an uplifted internal state; I feel myself called by a mysterious and higher voice.

In our contemporary pluralistic world, where a cross-cultural communication has increasingly become a matter of necessity for global survival, a new consciousness is emerging. One of the major features of this new consciousness is going to be a non-sectarian spirituality. A universal spirituality is at the very root of all traditions, but is continually lost in theological exclusivism, or in scholastic partiality, or in evangelical enthusiasm, and needs to be rediscovered and restated anew again and again. Anybody who would approach a major work of a religious tradition with a global perspective, and with an effort to discover the universal truths in it, will aid the development of the new consciousness in the right direction.

Having been brought up in India, my psyche is naturally Indian in its early formation, without my being able to say exactly what that means in the present context. When I read The Gospel According to St. John, I am struck by many similarities with the Indian traditions, and, of course, by many differences. In trying to understand the Gospel, here and there I have found some Indian texts specifically helpful in bringing a new way of looking at a metaphor or in enlarging the appreciation of something that has already been understood. I am persuaded that the major division in the human psyche is not horizontal or regional, dividing the Eastern from the Western soul; rather it is vertical and global, separating the few from the many, and the spiritual, inner, and symbolical way of understanding from the material, outer, and literal one — culturally as well as in each human soul. Still its a relevant fact that my whole vision has been shaped to some extent by the Indian culture, even though no individual is completely determined by his cultural background.

My understanding of the Hindu tradition is that it aims at sanatana dharma (eternal order), of which at its best is one representation, and that the tradition is most fulfilled only when it succeeds in leading one to the Truth beyond itself and beyond oneself, to experience It and become one with it. One is born prakjita (natural, common, unformed); one must attempt to die samskrjita (well-sculpted, cultured, educated). The truly educated person, the formation of which is the real aim and meaning of any spiritual path, of any yoga, is he who is internally rightly *Bhagavad-Gita (6:29)*, "sees the Self in everyone, and everyone in the Self, seeing everywhere impartially." Everywhere, the one Truth and one Being, or simply the One, has manifested itself in many truths, myriad beings, and many selves, corresponding to different times, places, cultures, religious, and needs. Each language has its own particular genius, and some things can be expressed in it in a way which is especially profound and engaging; nevertheless no language has a monopoly on depth of discourse, nor does any particular language exhaust all possibilities of communication. In fact, at its best, as one sees in love, and in the utterances of so many mystics and sages, a language may most succeed as it carries one to the silence beyond any articulation. Similarly, each religious and spiritual tradition has its own beauty and emphasis, and certain truths are most profoundly expressed in it, and perhaps in it alone. Nevertheless, no tradition exhausts all possibilities of The Vastness, as no being exhausts all modalities of Being.

No two spiritual paths can be exactly the same, even though there may be many parallels and areas of agreement between them. Each path has its own specific center of gravity. And the most important thing from a practical religious point of view is to be actually searching for and responding to a way, a path of inner integration; that alone can lead to salvation or freedom or truth. Still even the practice of a path, and not only its theory, can be illumined by a light coming from another tradition. What is important to appreciate is that no spiritual path can be true if it is essentially devised here below by human reasoning. A true path depends on the Will of Heaven; it originates from Above. There cannot be a way from here to There, unless it be laid from There to here. In these matters, more than elsewhere, it is true as the Gospel says *(John 3:27)* that "A man can receive nothing, except it be given from heaven."

The way of Jesus Christ is through the Christ himself, that is to say, through the I which is "the only Son of God," which is "one with the Father," which is "the Word that was in the Beginning, with God, and was God" *(John 3:16, 10:30, 1:1)*. Having completely emptied himself of himself, so that the word we hear is not his and is instead the Word of the Father who sent him, *(John 14:24)*, having become a transmitting conduit without any personal distortions, he could say "the words that I speak unto you I speak not of myself: but the Father that dwelleth in me, he doeth the works." *(John 14:10)*. Such an I, in supreme identity with the Father, is the one which can say, "I am the way, the truth, and the life: no man cometh unto the Father, but by me." *(John 14:6)*. Whether the father had incarnated himself in the body of Jesus of Nazareth, or whether Jesus became one with the Father, is not necessary for us to resolve here, especially when we recall the Gospel saying that "no man hath ascended up to heaven, but he that came down from heaven" *(John 3:13)*.

However, it is important to guard against a lowering of the level of insight: the significant truth, which alone has the power to lead to eternal life, resides in the egoless supreme identity in which "the Father and I are one," and less in any exclusive identification of the Father with this specific person or that. In the Indian tradition, particularly in the Upanisads, the deepest Self of every human being, the very kernel of a person, the Atman, is said to be beyond any limiting particularity, and identically one with Brahman, the Absolute, the essence of all there is. Furthermore, the way to Brahman is through the Atman. This is equally true in the *Bhagavad-Gita*, where the overall mode of discourse is much closer in its theistic metaphor to that in the gospels: Krishna, the incarnate God, repeatedly says that he is seated in the heart of everyone, and a person can come to know him and participate in his being by following his own essential being. Anyone who speaks from that core of oneself, which is possible only when one has surrendered all of one's relatively superficial selves to the service of this one Self, constitutes a bridge, a way, from here to There.

The way, however, is not the goal; and a person can too easily get excessively attached to a particular way or a teacher. Especially when someone is against other teachers and other ways, he commits a sin against the Holy Spirit in limiting its possibilities to only one mode of expression which he has somehow, usually by an accident of birth in a particular culture, encountered. Thus one practices idolatry in another form even though one may be against idols of other people. The ever present sense of exclusivism of the way and the savior, so pervasive in Christianity, is in my judgment based on a misunderstanding of the sacred texts, by interpreting at the surface what is spoken from the depth, and is not worthy of Jesus Christ who completely denied his self, and emptied himself of any feeling of particularity, as well as distinction from God. "And a certain ruler asked him, saying 'Good Master, what shall I do to inherit eternal life?' And Jesus said unto him, "Why callest thou me good? None is good, save one, that is, God.'" *(Luke 18:18-19)*.

In addition to the point of view implied in the remarks above, this study is written with certain further assumptions and attitudes, which together specify what may be called the method of vertical reasoning.

The first assumption is that the Gospel According to St. John is not on test. If anyone or anything is on test, it is we ourselves and our sensitivity. The text has proved itself: many times, in many places and to many very intelligent and sensitive people. It constitutes one of the most sacred texts of a great religion, and has provided spiritual nourishment to an entire culture over centuries. If it does not speak to us, alas! too bad for us! It is not for nothing that so many great teachers have said words to the effect that "you have ears but do not hear; you have eyes but do not see." If we cannot hear we must surely be hardened and closed of heart, and in a defensive posture of narrow-mindedness. There are some people in whom such a posture has been formed in reaction to the extreme insensitivity and bellicose aggression of some others who proclaim adherence or opposition to the Gospel and its message. Still, if one can be a little freed of such reactions, the beauty of the Gospel will be apparent.

The second assumption is that the Gospel has come down to us from a higher mind than ours. If there is something in it which we do not understand, the difficulty is likely to be in us and in our limitations. One cannot be blind to the fact that there are several places where the later editors, compilers, translators, and others with various interests have added words or stories to the Gospel which change the original meaning or intention. This was perhaps done sometimes unintentionally and sometimes with a view to a doctrinal dispute. But in our attempts to make some sense of the text, whenever there is any question about its intelligence, we have no doubt that the Gospel comes from a higher intelligence than ours. In fact, precisely at the point where our best efforts do not yield a satisfactory sense in the Gospel, there is an opportunity for us to listen with quietness and humility so that we may hear what we are not usually accustomed to hear, and allow the Gospel to work its magic in lifting us above ourselves. I am convinced that the scriptures and the teachers are not among us in order to be intelligible to us while we remain as we are; on the contrary, I believe that they are here so that we may become higher than we ordinarily are. All religions everywhere insist that we do not live as we might: from our right mind. Thus we live in sin, or in sorrow or in illusion or in a dream-like sleepy state; and not in grace, with joy, in reality, wakeful. The teachings from Above, of which the scriptures are an example, cannot be for the purpose of adding more knowledge or comfort or dreams to our sleepy state; we assume that they can nudge us a little towards wakefulness if we do not undo their effect by dragging them down to our level, at which we win or lose theological arguments, convert others to our doctrines, and exercise control over them.

A true path depends on the will of Heaven. It originates from Above.

The third assumption is that the Gospel belongs to the whole world, and in particular to those who feel called by it and find some help in it, even though they are not nominally Christian and have no need of so labeling themselves. It is a great classic of world spirituality, and too important to be relegated to an exclusively sectarian reading. I detect a curious attitude among many of the Christians I have met, scholars and non-scholars alike. They find it a little odd that anybody who is not a Christian should be seriously reading Christian books. It is understandable to them that one might read such books to become a Christian, or even in order to engage in polemics against Christianity, but one must choose and take sides. Commitment to Christ seems to imply for them either an enthusiastic to mild commitment against other teachers and teachings, or a certain degree of tolerance and allowance for co-existence of other religious, but not very often any conviction that these other teachings could be useful for one's own salvation. And those Christians who find something of value in other teachings often find it necessary to put Christianity down and to deny that they are Christian. Perhaps this either/or attitude arises from an over-literal interpretation of a fragment of a saying of Jesus Christ, namely, "He that is not with me is against me" *(Matthew 12:30; Luke 11:23)*. For myself, I am happy to find light wherever I can, without thereby having to deny other sources of illumination or other colors of the spectrum, which together can more fully express the glory and abundance of The Vastness than any one can alone.

The fourth assumption is that there is a definite meaning to spiritual sensitivity, which perhaps all human beings have in a rudimentary form and which is highly developed in some. This spiritual sense is able to comprehend subtle ideas, suggestions, and phenomena which are not comprehensible to the other senses and the rational mind. To me it appears obvious that scholarship, erudition, and mental acumen by themselves are not sufficient for approaching the scriptures, although they justly have a high place, and could be most illuminating.

However, this extra dimension of spiritual sensitivity seems to be a much more important requirement. As is said in another tradition, just as a donkey bearing a sandalwood load knows its weight but not its fragrance, so also is a scholar who knows the texts of the scriptures but not their significance. It is clear, on the other hand, that ignorance of what scholarship has to say about any matter pertaining to the scriptures is by itself no guarantee of spiritual sensitivity! My interest in the gospel is not doctrinal or dogmatic in the ordinary sense of these words. Nevertheless, one may recognize and understand what Jesus the Christ said, "If any man will do his will, he shall know of the doctrine, whether it be of God, or whether I speak of myself" *(John 7:17)*.

There are many levels of quality of being Christian — from Jesus the Christ to Torquemada the inquisitor. In pointing to this wide variation my purpose is not to belittle Christianity or to elevate it; a similar qualitative range exists in every other religious tradition. My interest in this study is to discover a subtler and less churchly level in the Gospel than usual, to which many thoughtful and sensitive Christians, as well as non-Christians, are lost simply because there is not an appreciation of the various levels of being within each human being, and the corresponding levels within Christianity.

As one grows spiritually, it is natural and necessary to be free of the level of religion which one knows and in which one dwells; in clinging to that level, one accepts a stunting of the natural process of development. Unfortunately, far too often there is a fixed, externalistic notion of what Christianity is; and it does not permit people, especially disgruntled ex-Christians, to see the immense spiritual wealth of Christianity, and its dynamic elasticity adequate to the full measure of the most developed soul. Many years ago in one of my classes, while disputing an interpretation of one of the parables in the Gospels, an ordained minister of a Protestant church had pronounced that "Mysticism has nothing to do with Christianity; it is just a Catholic heresy." To be sure, he later regretted having made that remark, and wished to withdraw it because, as he said, he had spoken unconsciously. After the class, another participant, a Sufi Muslim and now quite a well-known professor of Religion, said to me with tears in his eyes, "How sad! So many Christians don't know what treasures there are in the gospels."

I write in hope of letting the inner Christ grow in us; for me it is a form of prayer and meditation. I am called by, and heartily endorse, what the 17th century mystic Angelus Silesius wrote:

> Christ could be born
> a thousand times in Galilee —
> but all in vain
> until He is born in me.

The Gospel According to St. John is different from the other gospels in its overall point of view concerning Jesus Christ and his mission on the earth. It is much more cosmological in scale and mystical in nature than the other canonical gospels which are all called the synoptic gospels owing to the fact that they, in contrast to John, can together be regarded as revealing the same vision. John's Gospel has been for a very long time considered as more inner or spiritual or esoteric. Clement of Alexandria (about 150-215 A.D.) said about it: "Last of all (meaning after the other evangelists) John, perceiving that the external facts had been made plain in the gospel, being urged by his friends, and inspired by the Spirit, composed a spiritual gospel."

It is not clear who was the author. The Church tradition for centuries has identified him with the Beloved Disciple mentioned in the Gospel itself, and him with John, son of Zebedee. It is doubtful that it was written by one of the apostles who witnessed the events himself; however, the Gospel may have been based on some eyewitness accounts which circulated orally for decades among a school of early Christians. The direct evidence, such as it is, regarding the time of its composition, points on the whole to a date between 80-120 A.D., after the other three gospels. However, this is not at all certain. It could have been written as early as 70 A.D., and could thus be the first gospel to be written.

Among the distinctive features of the Gospel According to St. John are two which may be remarked upon here. Much more than the other gospels, this one has a special propensity for highlighting contrasts: between light and darkness, between one who is from Above and one who is from below, between God and the world, between good and evil, between Spirit and flesh, and the like. Secondly, the author seems to be self-consciously setting out a parallel in many places between the *Old Testament* and the *New Testament*. For example, there is similar scale and style in the opening lines of the *Book of Genesis* and the present Gospel, and a complete parallel between the sacrifice of Jesus Christ as the Lamb of God and the lamb sacrificed by the Israelites at the Passover feast; as the latter has to do with physical freedom from bondage, the former with spiritual freedom from sin.

In general, John is much less concerned with the actual historical events in the life of Jesus Christ and more with his spiritual teachings. There is no mention at all about the birth of Jesus or his childhood, nor of his father Joseph. Although his mother is mentioned in the Gospel, she is never identified as Mary. The author is not particularly interested in such biographical or historical details. The first reference to Jesus Christ on the earth is the sighting of him by John the Baptist who immediately recognizes him as the Chosen One of God, and as the Lamb of God, previsioning his sacrifice for the sake of mankind.

There can be no doubt about the symbolic nature of the various events and miracles mentioned in this Gospel. Two of the most important miracles performed by Christ, namely the raising of Lazarus from the dead, and the transforming of water into wine at Cana, are not even mentioned in any of the other gospels. This is especially puzzling in the case of the former miracle: by any ordinary or literal standards the bringing of a dead person to life has to be considered the most stunning miracle of all, and one about which it is difficult to avoid public notice. But it may be briefly noted that there are ways of speaking about transformation of being and the forging of an internal integration so that those who were like the dead found a new and a more abundant life.

That such miracles may have actually and externally taken place, indicating the possession by Jesus Christ of supernatural powers, is entirely possible. Why not? We hardly know all there is to know about nature; and there may be principles and forces available only in heightened states of consciousness, as attested universally in all cultures. However, what interests me here is the greatest miracle of all: transformation of being. Rather than the external transformation of water into wine, what I find vastly more engaging is the fact that by the action of Christ, Saul could be internally transformed into Paul.

Soon after the descent of the Holy Spirit on his head, seen spiritually by John the Baptist, Jesus Christ begins to teach.

It is the teaching that engages John; and in this Gospel one finds mainly long discourses, and only a few short sayings or parables. The teaching of Jesus Christ exists for exactly the same purpose as do all other authentic teachings; to show mankind a way of transformation of being so that one may live not self-centered as one does but God-centered, The true teaching does not originate from this person or that, but only from God; and he alone who is with Him can reveal it. "My doctrine is not mine, but his that sent me" *(John 7:16)*.

According to the *Shatapatha Brahmana (1,7,2,1-5)*, when a man is born, simultaneously with him are born obligations to the Gods, to the sages, to the ancestors, and to the community of fellow men. Out of these, the obligation to the sages is met by studying the Veda (literally, sacred knowledge); this is how we repay our debts to them. Now we are living at a special moment in world history: for the first time it seems to be possible for us to be free from our cultural isolation, and to become heirs to the wisdom and truth as much of the Christ as of Lao Tze, of Krishna or of the Buddha, if we would. In the global village that we live in, as we have access to the words and teachings of more sages, our obligations are also increased. I hope to meet a part of my obligation to the Christian sages by studying the Gospel According to St. John, which represents the Christian Veda par excellence.

However, in paying our debts to the sages and the saints, we must not forget a yet higher obligation: that to the Vastness beyond. It is this that the sages behold and to which they themselves are beholden; they show us that the kingdom is neither in this place nor in that, but in each individual soul that is centered in the present moment on the only One who is.

As Christ said, "Woman, believe me, the hour cometh, when ye shall neither in this mountain, nor yet at Jerusalem, worship the Father. But the hour cometh, and now is, when the true worshipers shall worship the Father in spirit and in truth; for the Father seeketh such to worship him. God is a Spirit; and they that worship him must worship him in spirit and in truth." *(John 4:21, 23-34).*

(From the introduction to *The Fire of the Cross: The Teaching and the Practice in the Gospel According to St. John*, a work-in-manuscript by Ravi Ravindra. Copyright 1988 by Ravi Ravindra.)

RAVI RAVINDRA is the Chairman of the Department of Religions at Dalhousie University in Halifax, where he is also an Adjunct Professor of Physics. Born in India, he has lived in Canada since 1961. He has written widely on science and comparative religion and is the author of *Whisper From the Other Shore: Spiritual East and West.*

HEALING, REMISSION AND MIRACLE CURES

A lecture by Brendan O'Regan

I'd like to begin by reviewing a little of the history of the projects I'll be telling you about later in my talk. Those of you who are familiar with the Institute of Noetic Sciences know that we've sponsored a lot of work involving the mind/body relationship and its importance in health. During the 1970s, for example, we supported research of people like Carl and Stephanie Simonton, who were working with terminal cancer patients using psychotherapeutic techniques, meditational and guided imagery approaches and biofeedback to demonstrate that the mind/body relationship was indeed important and could affect the course of illness and disease. In 1975 people thought this kind of work was highly unusual. The general climate was one in which this kind of mind/body link wasn't well understood and many, many people expressed doubt that the link even existed in a way that had any significant effect on health. Some people were less than polite and told us that we were crazy for supporting this kind of work.

But it's been interesting to see what has happened in the years since then. I remember a discussion with Carl and Stephanie back in 1976 when we were speculating where in the mind/body system psychological factors could have an impact. They said that their best guess was the immune system. There was no field then of psychoneuroimmunology, which has emerged in just the past five or six years. This field, as many of you know, is concerned with the links between the mind, the brain and the immune system and how they communicate with each other. It is through this system that psychological factors do indeed seem to have an impact on health and disease.

Although we didn't know this was the case back in the '70s when we supported these projects, we knew intuitively we were on the right track. There was enough anecdotal evidence to justify exploring this area. Today we are heavily immersed in this approach. And something else has happened as well. In the early 1980s we at Noetic Sciences realized that while we had been funding practitioners of alternative techniques in medicine who demonstrated effects, we weren't really looking into the mechanisms of these effects. We weren't getting at how the connection between mind and body is mediated, or "What are the mediating pathways?" as the question would be asked in scientific circles today.

So we started a program called the Inner Mechanisms of the Healing Response. One of the premises of the program is based on the observation that in medicine, or in science generally, progress occurs when it is recognized that certain seemingly disconnected things are acting together and forming a system. For example the circulatory system, the nervous system and the immune system were not recognized as systems until people gradually realized that they were indeed working in coordination as systems.

The Placebo Effect

We noticed that there were a lot of sporadic data "all over the map" about healing. Take, for example, the placebo effect in medicine. The placebo effect is one of those annoying things, from some points of view in medicine, that says that some people — approximately 35-40 percent — will get better when they take a "sugar pill" or an inert substance they are told is a drug that will help them. Some of their responses can be fairly modest, such as the relief of pain. Many people say, though, the pain is a subjective phenomenon or psychosomatic; so they're not terribly impressed by that result. Other examples are more dramatic. For example, in the 1950s it was common to perform a certain kind of surgery to relieve the pain of angina pectoris. At that time some experiments were performed which could not get by a Human Subjects Review Committee today, I assure you. In these experiments patients with that disease were cut open and then simply sewn back up again. The operation -- a sham operation if you like — took place and the patients were then sewn back together. Those patients reported just as much relief from angina pectoris as the people who'd had the full surgery. So it turns out that surgery for angina pectoris produced a placebo effect.

There's another intriguing example from the World Journal of Surgery, which reported on the test of a new kind of chemotherapy in 1983. As is often the case in such tests, there was an experimental group that received chemotherapy, and a control group that received a sugar pill or an inert substance. One of the effects of chemotherapy that we're all familiar with is hair loss — so people expect to lose their hair when given chemotherapy. In this study 30 percent of the control group — given placebos -- lost their hair. That's a very physical effect! There's got to be some kind of mediating pathway for it. In fact, it's been named the "nocebo" effect, as opposed to the placebo effect which means "I shall please". This is not pleasing!

So those who think of placebos as having only modest, inconsequential and subjective effects should look at some of these data because there definitely are direct physical effects of placebos. In fact less kind people say that the history of medicine is the history of the placebo effect, at least until the discovery of drugs or antibiotics, because many of the substances that were administered before the 1930s have since been found to be pharmacologically inactive or ineffective.

But even recently within the realm of chemotherapy there are interesting effects. Dr. Bernard Siegel of Yale told me a story about a chemotherapeutic agent called cis-platinum. When cis-platinum came out, it was greeted with a great deal of enthusiasm. Doctors were getting 75 percent effectiveness from administering cis- platinum to their patients. But over time, doctors further removed from the initial enthusiasm would administer chemotherapy in a sort of "ho-hum" routine way, and the effectiveness rate dropped down to about 25-30 percent.

Given these physical effects of placebos, one wonders what can be going on. There must be complex pathways between mind and body indeed belief systems.

Multiple Personality

Then we at the Institute started investigating another phenomenon which had intrigued me for some time — multiple personality, which is exhibited by people who have been severely physically abused, even sexually, as children. Dr. Frank Putnam of the National Institutes of Health (NIH), one of the country's experts on that subject, has found that electroencephalograms (EEGs) of people who go from one personality to another will change as dramatically as though the electrodes had been taken off one person and placed on another. The difference in brain activity is that great. Most intriguing is that some of these people will be allergic to a drug in one personality and not allergic to it in another. Some cases have been reported of women who've had three menstrual periods each month because they had three different personalities, each one with its own cycle. A more peculiar situation that I have difficulty accepting — I've heard of four cases, but I've never witnessed one — is that of eye color changing between personalities.

What all of this implies is that there is an extraordinary plasticity in the relationship between mind and body. It's very interesting to examine this in multiples because it involves the same biology, the same genetics, the same physical being. Some, by the way, take the view that there is a connection between temporal lobe epilepsy and multiple personality; they say that completely different brain regions are being activated, so different sets of instructions are being sent out. But indeed, isn't that what we want to happen when we're trying to get someone to change illness in the direction of healing? Following this line of reasoning we decided to fund a study at NIH — it's ironic that Noetic Sciences gives money to NIH — to examine the immune systems of multiples while they change personalities. This study, which had not been done before, is now being conducted by Dr. Putnam in collaboration with Dr. Nicholas Hall at George Washington Medical School. As all of this began to gel in my mind I thought, well, maybe there is something in addition to a nervous system and an immune system and an endocrine system — something like a healing system. Maybe it is a system that doesn't manifest unless challenged. Maybe it's a system that can lie dormant until confronted with stress, trauma, disease or illness of some kind. If that was so, then it would explain why it just isn't an obvious part of ourselves. As I was speculating along these lines, and about a year after I had written some notes about this, I found a statement from Norman Cousins in his book *Human Options*. He says:

> Over the years, medical science has identified the primary systems of the human body, the circulatory system, digestive system, endocrine system, autonomic nervous system, parasympathetic nervous system, and the immune system. But two other systems that are central to the proper functioning of a human being need to be emphasized. The healing system, and the belief system. The two work together. The healing system is the way the body mobilizes all its resources to combat disease. The belief system is often the activator of the healing system.

So I found I was not alone in thinking this way. We then asked ourselves, "How would we maximize the evidence of this healing system?" After all, this is not an accepted point of view; it's not taught in medical schools, I'm sure. We decided to look into a subject of which I'd heard rumors and anecdotal evidence for years -- spontaneous remission.

Spontaneous Remission

Spontaneous remission is a phenomenon with a very curious history in medicine. The majority view is that spontaneous remission doesn't really happen — that it is, in fact, an artifact of misdiagnosis. According to this view the person never really had that disease, they had something else. If this turns out to be the case, then we should know the extent of it in medicine and attempt to get rid of it.

However, the dictionary definitions of "spontaneous" and "remission" are intriguing. The word "spontaneous" means "acting in accordance with, or resulting from feeling, temperament or disposition, or from a native internal proneness, readiness or tendency without compulsion, constraint or premeditation." Another meaning is "acting by its own impulse, energy, or natural law without external cause or influence." "Remission" means "the act of remitting, a natural releasing, resigning or relinquishing, surrendering. Forgiveness, pardon as of sins or crimes." There are some very interesting messages locked up in those words, so I thought we should look at the literature on remission to see what we might learn about the dynamics of the phenomenon.

It turns out, however, that there are no existing texts on the subject. Remission simply is not a subject a physician or a researcher can look up in the library, at least not yet. There are only two books on the topic, one by Everson and Cole on 176 cases of regression of cancer (but that book is out of print and one of the authors is dead); and the other by William Boyd on regression of cancer (also out of print and the author is deceased). There is only one document that you can get your hands on, which is a report on a conference that took place twelve years ago at Johns Hopkins University, available from the National Cancer Institute.

So a year ago we got busy on our computers and started going into the databases, and we have now assembled over 3000 articles from over 860 medical journals in over 20 different languages. By the way, one article can be about as many as several hundred cases. As far as I know this is the largest compilation of data on spontaneous remission in the world. We will be publishing our work on this early next year, and have already completed a draft of the first volume, which is entitled Remission with No Allopathic Intervention. Some very interesting pictures emerge from this.

First of all, we have found cases of remission from almost every kind of illness, not just cancer. We've selected about 800 of the most striking examples of spontaneous remission — out of 3000 articles — for inclusion in volume one of the spontaneous remission bibliography. We have many cases of remission with no medical intervention at all. These are the purest ones, the ones that give us the strongest evidence that there is an extraordinary self-repair system lying dormant within us. These make up about one-fifth of what we have collected. Then if you go to the cases where there's inadequate medical treatment, in other words something was done for the person, but they did not receive a treatment that would be expected to cure them in any way — for example, a biopsy is not considered curative — then you get about twice as many articles. It's fascinating to look at what you find. We're prepared an abstract for every one of these papers and have put all this information in an electronic database. We've also extracted some case histories. What you find in these histories is fascinating. I would like to give you some examples of the kinds of things we've found because when you hear actual cases you get a very good feel for what can happen.

Let me say that many of the people who write these medical journal reports do so with a great sense of apology, because they seem to be saying to their colleagues, "Well, we really did diagnose this correctly; we thought the x-rays might have gotten misplaced so we took them again; and we definitely found that this person really had the disease." Then you get the same story all over again when they go through the remission. In effect, they are saying: "The disease really did disappear. We re-did the tests several times and to our amazement, the tumor was completely gone."

Here's a case from *The Journal of Thoracic and Cardiovascular Surgery*, 1954, a case of spontaneous regression of an untreated bronchiogenic carcinoma. If you'll bear with me through the technical detail in the following report, I think it will give you some sense of how thorough these reports are.

A fifty-nine year old white man was admitted to the George Washington

University Hospital on May 19, 1947. The patient had been in good health until September of 1946 when he first noticed an increase in a chronic cough which he had had for years. In addition, he gave a history of malaise and increasing dyspepsia of two months' duration, and an eighteen pound weight loss over a period of six months, The patient suffered from chronic bronchitis of about twenty years' duration. He had smoked from two to three packages of cigarettes daily for many years. X-rays of the chest revealed an opacity in the right lung field at the level of the third and fourth intercostal spaces anteriorly. On July 20, a right thoracotomy was performed which revealed a carcinoma of the lung with involvement of the right helium and invasion of the mediastinum at the level of the inferior pulmonary artery. A biopsy of the mass was taken and since the lesion appeared inoperable, the chest was closed. Microscopic examination of the tissue revealed epidermoid carcinoma.

During the post-operative period, x-rays of the chest revealed progressive clearing of the pulmonary lesion in the right lung. This became particularly apparent about six months after the exploratory thoracotomy. The incredible behavior of the pulmonary lesion naturally aroused suspicion that there had been a mistake made in the histologic diagnosis and perhaps a mislabeled specimen accounted for an erroneous diagnosis. Accordingly, new sections were made which again revealed epidermoid carcinoma.

The patient was readmitted to the hospital May 19, 1952, exactly five years after the original admission. A careful re- evaluation of his entire life history was undertaken to obtain any pertinent facts which could have influenced the behavior of the lung cancer. Nothing of significance could be found except that for four or five years he had been employed as a linotype operator with exposure to noxious fumes. This ultimately led him to change his occupation. (This is all you now hear about the patient as a person.)

Following the operation in 1947, he took two halibut liver oil capsules daily for a considerable period of time, four vegetable compound tablets daily, an occasional barbiturate for sleep and vitamin B-1 tablets. The vegetable compound tablets were analyzed and were found to contain asparagus, parsley, watercress and broccoli. The almost complete disappearance of the lesion in the right lung was constant, corresponding to x-rays of the past four years.

Notice that this patient was operated on and a biopsy was taken. However, no attempt was made to remove the tumor since it was regarded as inoperable. This is categorized as "no allopathic intervention" from a technical standpoint — though when one learns that biopsy procedures alone can appear to stimulate remissions, one wonders if this categorization will remain appropriate.

Emerging Patterns

I could quote many more of these cases but for brevity I'll tell you just a few of the patterns we've seen in the literature. One of the patterns is that you rarely hear anything of the patients as persons — what they believe, what they do, what they feel. It's just not included. That's understandable in the context of the time that these papers were written and the attitude in medicine then. But when you read enough of them, after a while you start to notice a mounting symphony of the absence of the person. I remember one paper by a Dr. Weinstock in New York about a woman who had cervical cancer that had metastasized throughout her body. She was considered beyond treatment and beyond help. As the paper continued it said, "And her much-hated husband suddenly died, whereupon she completely recovered." So you say to yourself — wait a minute, shouldn't we follow up these kinds of things? One is left wondering what might be behind that kind of statement.

Another pattern we noticed — quite independently of another research group that we later discovered had been following the same thing — is that many patients who go into remission had an infection at a certain point along the way. It might have been a bacterial infection, often some kind of skin infection, and it will be noted in the report that the infection caused a fever to which there was a reaction and then the fever subsided and slowly the tumor disappeared. We thought this was rather interesting. As we went back in time (you can go back electronically in the databases to 1966, but after that you're on your own in the old-fashioned way in the library) we finally got back to the twenties and teens and we began to notice more reports of this kind of remission. We tracked these reports of remission following bacterial infections to a man named Dr. William Coley of New York. He noticed back in the 1890's that his patients who became infected with a bacterial skin infection called erysipelas would react with a fever and spend a few days fighting it off — as though the immune system were being activated to fight off the infection.

Then in about 40 percent of the patients, the cancer would disappear. Coley turned this around and started giving people infections, infecting them directly with erysipelas in order to stimulate their immune systems; he did indeed achieve an interesting success rate.

But in 1935, when Coley died, chemotherapy and x-ray treatments for cancer began, and infection techniques seemed old-fashioned and no longer relevant. His daughter, Helen Coley Nauts, still alive at about 80 years old in New York City, told me recently that since she believed her father was doing something important, she had gone to a friend, Lloyd Old at Sloan-Kettering, and said "What can I do to have this work taken seriously?" Old told her, "Gather a hundred cases, well-documented, fully detailed medical histories and bring them to me. I'll distribute them to my colleagues and we'll see." She came back with 1000 cases! Out of that came an organization in

New York, Cancer Research Institute, founded by Coley's daughter to pursue this line of research. Just as a footnote, Old began to look into what it was erysipelas infection stimulated in animal systems, and this is how tumor necrosis factor was discovered; this was then cloned by Genentech and is now in clinical trial at Sloan-Kettering. So you have an interesting consequence of a very physical sort in the study of the kinds of systems involved in remission.

Our Remission Project has uncovered other interesting work in many other countries. We have about 250 papers in other languages, including Japanese, Swedish, German, Italian and Hebrew. In Sweden and Japan researchers have been removing plasma from people in remission, particularly with metalogic (blood) diseases, and have been injecting it into other people and, in some cases, are getting remission; this suggests there are blood-borne factors that I believe can one day be isolated from people in remission. This is yet another reason to gather data on these people.

Another quite different aspect of remission is the cases reported involving psychological and spiritual phenomena. Here is part of a report from a very interesting Australian physician, Ainslie Meares, who unfortunately died in September of this year. This case involved the regression of osteogenic sarcoma metastasis associated with intensive mediation.

> The patient, aged twenty-five, underwent a mid-thigh operation for osteo-genic sarcoma eleven months before he first saw me, two and one-half years ago. (This report was written in 1978.) He had visible bony lumps of about two centimeters in diameter growing from the ribs, sternum and the crest of the ilium and was coughing up small quantities of blood in which he said he could feel small pieces of bone.

> There were gross opacities in the x-ray films of his lungs. The patient had been told by a specialist that he had only two or three weeks to live, but in virtue of his profession he was already well aware of the pathology and prognosis of his condition. Now, two and one-half years later, he has moved to another state to resume his former occupation. This young man has an extraordinary will to live and has sought help from all the alternatives to orthodox medicine which were available to him. These have included acupuncture, massage, several sessions with Phillipine faith healers, laying-on of hands, and yoga at an Indian ashram. He had short sessions of radiation therapy and chemotherapy, but declined to continue. (This would be classified more as a case of inadequate treatment in technical terms.) He also persisted with the dietary and enema treatment described by Max Gerson, the German physician who gained some notoriety for this type of treatment in American in the 1940s. However in addition to all these measures to gain relief, the patient has consistently

maintained a rigorous discipline of intensive meditation. He has, in fact, consistently meditated from one to three hours daily. Two other factors seem to be important. (Meares, by the way, is one researcher who describes more about the patient and not as much about the disease.)

He has had extraordinary help and support from his girlfriend who more recently became his wife. She's extremely sensitive to his feelings and needs and has spent hours in aiding his meditation and healing with massage and laying-on of hands. The other important factor would seem to be the patient's own state of mind.

He has developed a degree of calm about him which I have rarely observed in anyone, even in Oriental mystics with whom I have had considerable experience. When asked to what he attributes the regression of metastases, he answers in some such terms as "I really think it is our life, the way we experience our life." In other words, it would seem that the patient has let the effects of the intense and prolonged meditation enter into his whole experience of life. His extraordinary low level of anxiety is obvious to the most casual observer. It is suggested that this has enhanced the activity of his immune system by reducing his level of cortisol.

So some clues come occasionally from people who are studying the mind/body relationship in relation to remission. But by far the largest number of cases do not involve this kind of information. You're simply told that people survived — period. In 1985 we went to the National Tumor Registry, which is operated by the National Cancer Institute. This Registry has eleven centers around the country, which keep track of all the incidents of tumors. If a patient goes to a hospital and cancer is diagnosed, the Tumor Registry is informed of the type of tumor, the patient's age, race, sex, and various other details. That's how the records on the incidence of cancer are built up. They don't track remission, however, and they don't even really track long-term survival anymore. But even so I went to the San Francisco Bay Area Tumor Registry, which covers the five Bay Area counties, and I said "Look, we're interested in remission." They said, "No, no, we don't have information on that here." And I said, "Well, how long do you keep track of patients? Do you keep track of them for five years, or ten years?" They said, "We keep track of them until they die." I said, "Oh? In that case, you could look for long-term survivors." They said, "Yes, we could." Their database had been computerized in 1973, and I was talking to them in 1985, so I said "Well, why don't we look in your records for people who were told between 1973 and 1975 that they had terminal cancer, that it was not just cancer at a primary site, that it had metastasized throughout their body. Look in your records now in 1985 and see if any of them are still alive." They said, "Fine, we can do that very easily." They went into the database and came back with 100 names: 100 people still alive ten years past a terminal diagnosis. We agreed that we'd better make sure these people were still alive; you know, this whole issue of just exactly when people are really dead is rather tricky because some people are still trying to collect social security, and there are strange things involving insurance claims. This is a kind of netherworld I hadn't penetrated before. They said "We will verify that they are all alive."

They were then successful in verifying that 89 of these individuals were still alive. These people all had different kinds of cancer. What startled me the most was there were two cases of pancreatic cancer, which is normally very lethal. So we are now attempting to get the release of their names and permission to talk to them.

Talking to somebody in remission can be a very delicate process. We learned this when two women in remission came to visit us. (By the way, I can't verify this statistically, but we seem to hear of more women than men in remission.) One of these women came to talk to Caryle Hirshberg, my associate who has been doing our database search. She looked at Caryle somewhat suspiciously and said "You're not a doctor, are you? I don't want to talk to a doctor!" Caryle said, "No, I'm not. Really, honest." Then she said, "Well, I just don't want to be put down and turned away again, like I was so many times. I'm going to keep my state of mind intact, no matter what."

Unfortunately this has been what we've found frequently with the few people we've talked to -- they've been turned away. I very much like what Yale surgeon Bernard Siegel, author of *Love, Medicine and Miracles*, says about this problem, "Talk to your patients. Never turn them away. Because even if you don't agree with what they're doing, they'll still come back and tell you about it." And the fact is that most people with remissions don't come back and tell anybody. At least, they don't tell their doctors. You will see cases in our files of people who were seen ten years later in the hospital for something else and the physician says, "My God, I thought you were dead! You were in here ten years ago for something. How comes you're still alive?" So they sort of have to apologize, I guess.

You can see, it's a very complex business. But we thought we'd go a little further with this. I want to describe one other piece that has emerged as a curious pattern. I mentioned it earlier. We haven't analyzed this yet so I don't know what we'll do about it. One of the things that Caryle Hirshberg noticed was that when people who had kidney cancer had the kidney removed, the metastases from the kidney to the lung — the pulmonary metastases to the lung -- would frequently disappear. This is not considered terribly surprising. You're removing the primary site of the cancer and so maybe it is not so strange that the area to which the cancer had spread would heal. But then we began to notice that when some patients simply had a biopsy of the kidney, their pulmonary metastases would disappear. In these cases there is no surgery to remove the cancer. Only the amount captured by a needle biopsy is removed. So there's some interesting relationship between the kidney and the lung and the simple act of biopsy. That's not a technically "clean" remission, but it says that biopsy can

Resources

be part of the process of inducing remission somehow. When you intervene in one area, it sets up a process which can help in another. In a sense that is parallel to the infection cases.

Spiritual and Miraculous Healing

Going further, we then began to say, "We've heard for many years about claims of spiritual healing or miraculous healing.

We see these claims televised every night. What about these cases? Are these remissions or something else?" I thought I should look into this in order to have a more complete perspective of the whole field. So I asked myself first, "Where will this have been documented in some way that I can make sense of?" Anecdotal claims are important because they tell us there is a territory to be investigated, but they are not evidence, really. Then I thought about Lourdes, in France, where an apparition of the Virgin Mary appeared in 1858.

Since then there have been approximately 6000 claims of miraculous healing. Mind you, there have been millions of people going there, only 64 have made it through the procedures of the International Medical Commission to be officially declared miracles. The Commission was organized in a fairly sophisticated form in 1947, and they have records since about the 1860s, varying in quality during the early period.

Let me tell you a little bit about the Commission's procedure, so you'll realize that it is not easy to have a miracle, at least from their point of view. I am quoting here from a paper by St. John Dowling in the Journal of the Royal Society of Medicine of August 1984:

> At present there are 25 members of the Commission: thirteen French, two Italian, two Belgian, two English, two Irish, one each from Spain, Holland, Scotland and Germany. (Interestingly there are no members from the United States. I wonder about that.) Then they have a wide spread of specialties. Four each from general medicine and surgery, three from orthopedics, two each from general psychiatry and general practice, and one each from radiology, neuropsychiatry, dermatology, opthamology, pediatrics, cardiology, oncology, neurology and biochemistry. Ten members hold chairs in their medical schools. All are practicing Catholics. Many are doctors who come regularly to Lourdes as pilgrimage medical officers, but some have little or no connection with the shrine.
>
> If, after the initial scrutiny and follow- up, the Medical Bureau thinks that there is good evidence of an inexplicable cure, the dossier is sent to the International

Medical Commission which usually meets once a year in Paris. The preliminary investigation of the data is made, and if the members agree that the case is worth investigating, they appoint one or two of their members to act as rapporteur. The rapporteur then makes a thorough study of the case, usually seeing the patient himself (or herself), and presents the material in a detailed written dossier circulated to the members before the meeting at which they will make their decision.

The report is then discussed critically, at length, under 18 headings, a vote being taken at each stage. In the first three stages, the Committee considers the diagnosis and has to satisfy itself that a correct diagnosis has been made and proven by the production of the results of full physical examination, laboratory investigations, x-ray studies and endoscopy and biopsy where applicable. Failure at this stage is common because of inadequate investigation or missing documents. At the next two stages, the Committee must be satisfied that the disease was organic and serious without any significant degree of psychological overlay (their words).

Next it must make sure that the natural history of the disease precludes the possibility of spontaneous remission. (In other words, they throw out all cases where a remission could have occurred because, for them, remission is natural, not supernatural. Their rejects become part of our database. Hence the importance of talking to them.) The medical treatment given cannot have affected the cure. Cases ruled out here are those about which there cannot be any certainty that the treatment has not been effective. For example, a course of cytotoxic drugs would lead to the case being rejected even where the likelihood of success was small. (So they're operating with a fairly tough set of criteria.) Then the evidence that the patient has indeed been cured is scrutinized and the Committee must be satisfied that both objective and subjective symptoms have disappeared and that investigations are normal. The suddenness and completeness of the cure are considered together with any sequelae. Finally, the adequacy of the length of follow-up is considered. After this detailed study, the question, "Does the cure of this person constitute a phenomenon which is contrary to the observations and expectations of medical knowledge and scientifically inexplicable?" is put. A simple majority carries the case one way or the other.

This then gives you some idea of the criteria being used at Lourdes. It suggests quite careful scrutiny of the claims. It is also worth noting that they discard a large number of cases that perhaps should be included if there were better objective means of documenting them. I am referring here to the cases with significant psychological overlay, as Dowling points out. If you look at the chart describing all the cures at Lourdes since 1858, you find interesting changes in the data over time. For example, at the beginning there are many references to tuberculosis of various kinds. These no longer appear today since we now can cure TB. A skeptic will of course cast doubt on the accuracy of the diagnoses of some of the earlier cures and maybe this is correct in some cases. I think it is fair to say that doctors back in the 1860s probably did know how to diagnose things like TB and that they could easily have been wrong in diagnosing various types of cancer, cysts of the liver and so on. But when you come up to the present time those kinds of objections should diminish to a marked degree — particularly in the cases since 1947 when more modern procedures were instituted.

I want to deal with one case in some detail so you get a feeling for what goes on in the more contemporary cases. First though, here is a little quote from a paper by James Hansen that appeared in *New Scientist* in 1982, entitled "Can Science Allow Miracles?"

> A miracle is when something that cannot happen does anyway. It is not a question of the manifestation of hitherto unknown natural laws, if there are such that multiply loaves and permit walking on water, but rather a temporary suspension of nature itself by some outside supernatural action.

> If this can happen, there is a problem. In science, exceptions do not prove the rule. Doing research at all means making at least a few basic assumptions: that nature in knowable, and that is constant. Experiments can be done, and most important repeated.

> The genuine possibility of divine intervention as an unknown variable knocks the whole house of cards to pieces.

Let's see what you think of this particular house of cards with respect to the case I have chosen to go into in some detail. This is a man named Vittorio Michelli. I will now quote from the official report of the Medical Commission:

> He was admitted in 1962 to the Military Hospital of Verona in Italy suffering from a large mass in the buttock region limiting the normal range of movement of his left hip with leg and sciatic pain. After various unsuccessful therapeutic trials, radiological examination showed a structural alteration of the left iliac bone (osteolysis of the inferior half of the ilian bone and of the acetabular roof, amputation of the two rami of the ischium and gross osteoporosis of the femoral head) immediately suggestive of a malignant type of neoplastic lesion.

> At the end of May a biopsy was taken. The exposure of the tumor had to be made beneath the buttock muscles and the various sections revealed that the

specimen under consideration was a fusiform cell carcinoma. The sick man was them immobilized in a frame from pelvis to feet and sent during the month of June to a Centre for radiotherapy. Four days later he was discharged — without having received any therapy at all — and readmitted to the Military Hospital in Trente.

There during the next ten months there was no specific treatment, medical, surgical or radiotherapeutic, in spite of the fact that there was radiological evidence of persistent bony destruction; progressive loss of all active movement of the left lower limb; progressive deterioration. (In fact, the whole hip was being destroyed by the bone; it was being eaten away. He was literally falling apart — the leg was being separated, this mass was growing, and the actual bone of the pelvis was disintegrating.)

On the 24th of May, 1963 (this is now approximately a year after his original diagnosis) the patient left for Lourdes where he was bathed, in his plaster, several times.

One thing that happens at Lourdes is that people who go there are bathed in the spring. Some cynics say that the major miracle in Lourdes is that nobody has ever gotten sick from drinking the water in which these thousands of people have been bathed.

Upon bathing he had sudden sensations of heat moving through his body, which characterizes this kind of healing. We're not sure what it means, but you hear about it. When he arrived at Lourdes he couldn't eat and had lost vast amounts of weight. This information is all included in the report. After being bathed he felt an immediate return of his appetite and an amazing resurgence of energy. They took him back to the hospital, and frankly no one believed he felt better. Even people who let you go to Lourdes don't believe that it does anything, I guess! He started to gain weight and to be much more active. After about a month, his doctors finally consented to take his cast off and take another x-ray. They made an extensive report on what they found. In essence, they discovered that the tumor was getting smaller and smaller. It was regressing.

Then the tumor disappeared, and the bone began to regrow and completely reconstruct itself. Michelli was able to walk again two months after his return from Lourdes. I'll quote here from the report:

> A remarkable reconstruction of the iliac bone and cavity has taken place. The x-rays made in 1964, -5, -8 and -9 confirm categorically and without doubt that an unforeseen and even overwhelming bone reconstruction has taken place of a type unknown in the annals of world medicine. We ourselves, during

a university and hospital career of over 45 years spent largely in the study of tumors and neoplasms of all kinds of bone structures and having ourselves treated hundreds of such cases, have never encountered a single spontaneous bone reconstruction of such a nature.

At the end of this report they say,

Definitely a medical explanation of the cure of sarcoma from which Michelli suffered was sought and none could be found. He did not undergo specific treatment, did not suffer from any susceptible intercurrent infection that might have had any influence on the evolution of the cancer. (Notice here that they are aware that infections can stimulate remission.)

A completely destroyed articulation was completely reconstructed without any surgical intervention. The lower limb which was useless became sound, the prognosis is indisputable, the patient is alive and in a flourishing state of health nine years after his return from Lourdes.

There are 64 of these cases if you want to go into some detail, but I thought I'd pick just one and tell you about it.

There was a very intriguing paper published in the *Journal of the Royal Society of Medicine* in August of 1984. The author, St. John Dowling, did a follow-up study of thirteen of the people who had been cured at Lourdes. Nobody ever seems to talk to these people, and in contrast, I think I should jump on a plane and go interview them all! Of the thirteen, he found that eleven were still alive and well and healed, showing no signs of their original illness. Of the other two, one was dead because of a tractor accident. The other one is interesting because it tells you something about this whole question of our knowledge about remission. This was a woman who was recognized as having been cured in 1954. She had something called Bud-Chiari syndrome and its apparent disappearance was recognized as a miracle in 1963, but she died in 1970 from complications of that syndrome. They now have to go back and re-evaluate that and say "Well, we didn't know that she could go into temporary remission." It is a case where a decision was made, but it was really a temporary remission, not a complete cure. There's always this very difficult territory of distinguishing between a remission and a cure. I've heard "remission" referred to in certain major hospitals as simply "time to recurrence." The physicians will often say that it's inevitable, that it will recur. Maybe it will, maybe it won't.

It is worth noting that this commission has presumably the biggest database on remission outside of ours. Ours in now actually bigger that theirs, and as a result it turns out that we may be going to redefine how miracles are evaluated in the Catholic Church, to the extent that their definition of a miracle is dependent on the degree of their knowledge of remission. This, by the way, is not what I expected to do when I started the Remission Project.

At this point I thought to myself, here are these interesting healings occurring apparently as a result of an apparition that appeared in 1858. Is there anywhere today where an apparition might be appearing, and if there is, are there extraordinary healings associated with it? I discovered that there is indeed a site in Yugoslavia where an apparition of the Virgin Mary has been reported every day since June 24, 1981. It's in the little village of Medjugorje, about two-and- a-half hours north of Dubrovnik. I went there in May of 1986.

Now we read virtually nothing about this in the press here. There have been, to my knowledge, perhaps one or two articles.

It's interesting that *The New York Times* wrote about it in November of last year and referred to it as "Yugoslavia's little economic miracle" because they could only deal with the fact of the increasing tourism to Medjugorje. To be honest, that is a significant factor here because two million people have gone to this little village since 1981 just to be there. It's a major place of pilgrimage at this time.

I could talk to you for a long time about the apparition. Briefly, I learned there are six children, two boys and four girls, who see the apparition. It is not seen by everyone who is there. The purpose of the apparition, according to what it says to the children, is to bring peace to the world and to remind us of the need to become aware of God, in our own way. (These last four words are, by the way, making the Catholic hierarchy a little bit distracted because it doesn't suggest that everyone should become Catholic. Further there apparently was a bit of consternation in Medjugorje when a Moslem boy was healed.)

The children see this apparition every day around 6:30 to 6:45 pm. It doesn't matter where they are, but typically they gather together in a room to share the experience or to be there together. I interviewed two of them, one of the boys and one of the girls. Were they making this up? Are they credible? Did they seem to be presenting something that one could accept was an experience they were indeed having?

I won't go into a lot of detail now. However I became rapidly convinced that these were kids whose lives had been dramatically changed by the experience of the apparition in ways that made me feel that I would never want to exchange places with them. They have no privacy, for they are completely at the mercy of the millions of people going through there. They've been interrogated by the police, and the priest in charge has been put in jail and served eighteen months of a jail sentence. The authorities don't quite know what to make of this and they put roadblocks around the village every weekend and try to track who's coming and going. So it's a very complicated story.

I talked to the priest who was the children's spiritual director, Father Slavko, a Franciscan monk with a PhD in psychology — which is not what you'd expect in a little village in the middle of nowhere, so to speak. He was intrigued that I was there to study healing because nobody, or very few, had come for that purpose. Most people come to pray and to hear what the apparition has to say about the danger the world is in, the need for world peace, and all of these basic issues. I said, "Yes, I'm interested in all that too, but I want to know if there's healing happening here." And the answer was yes — there are some 250-300 reports. He let me see the various files. I noted that some of them were very good reports, some of them were very poor. So you don't regard this as much beyond anecdotal evidence.

One of the better cases was a woman from Milan, Italy, who had been diagnosed and treated under every kind of circumstance that you could imagine for multiple sclerosis. She arrived in a wheelchair, was in the apparition room with the children one evening, and while they were having the apparition experience, felt this sudden movement through her body and stood up and said, "I can walk, I am healed!" And the priest said, "Kneel down and pray." He just was not interested in the healing. She has since been in good health and her case is being monitored in Italy.

There have been cases of people with remission from blindness, from cancers, from tumors, from all sorts of things, and they are now beginning to send cases to the Medical Bureau at Lourdes, which isn't quite sure what to do with them. It's very intriguing that this sort of thing is going on and the Franciscan is quite circumspect. He's saying that in his view, he can sometimes tell who will be healed. I asked "What do you mean? How you can tell?" He said, "It's very often the people who come and don't determinedly want healing who are affected. They come with an open mind and with the spirit of simply doing God's will. They may ask for healing but they have not come with this as the single-minded purpose of their trip."

This suggested an interesting psychological profile of those that would be healed and indeed, being in Medjugorje presents one with an intense experiential sense of the presence of simple faith and devotion. Interestingly, one gets the impression that once can easily tell the difference between the devout and the merely pious there. There is a sad, faraway look in the eyes of the devout that is unmistakable. It seems like a kind of yearning for something, the search for a memory, the need for an all- embracing experience of love of a kind not ever found. This alone suggests to the eye seeking clues that these people are in a very different place psychologically, emotionally and indeed psychophysiologically.

I was in the apparition room with the children when they were having the experience of an apparition. I did not see the Virgin, in case you're wondering. But there was a very strange set of sensations that accompanied it. It was as though there was this incredible wave of feeling throughout the room that hit one in the solar plexus — an incredible kind of sadness that made people cry. It was a very intense thing that quietly takes hold of you. I was not told about that in advance, and I was sort of taken aback by it. It's all the more intense and curious because there are so many people outside the room, clamoring to get in. I felt guilty being there because there were people outside who had incredible problems who wanted to be in there, and then I was taking up space. But when the apparition left the children, everyone outside began spontaneously singing the Ave Maria in all these different languages with no cues from those inside the room as far as I could tell. So it's a strange feeling, but you get a sense that something very, very intense is happening there. To me it is more complex than any religious system. It's a very deep experience. You come away feeling, well, if there are conditions of prayer and spirit and mind that can be conducive to healing, then surely this is a good place for them to be expected.

So we have now in fact begun to try to study some of these people. We have some cooperation from an immunologist in Yugoslavia who may study some of them and do some tests. But it's difficult when you can't even write a letter there because of what the authorities might do. They have been known to confiscate equipment and forbid entry to people. It's a complicated story. I happened to be there, for example, when the cloud from Chernobyl blew over but we didn't even know it because we were cut off from the news. So I was startled when I later discovered that a researcher from Boston had gone there with some geiger counter equipment to measure radioactive levels, about two years ago. There were strange measurements on his geiger counter, way above the normal, when the apparition was appearing. One wonders just what that's about. He also measured the electrostatic field in the region where the apparition was appearing and noticed that it went up to about 70,000 volts per meter.

All kinds of studies have been made of the children, by the way. A team of French and a team of Italian doctors measured EEGs, and took electro-ocular scans. They've done everything to these poor kids while they were having an ecstatic experience of the Virgin. Somehow I didn't expect to react by feeling how ridiculous this seemed to be when one is actually there during such an event. An EEG is never going to capture an apparition, I don't think. But people were trying to do that.

There's a very interesting anecdote from another study that's going on. A doctoral student in Moscow, Idaho, put an ad in the paper asking if anybody in a 300-mile radius of that town had experienced a remission. She got twenty-five replies, and she started conducting interviews. Many who replied were farmers' wives. She asked one of them, "How did you feel when the doctor told you that you had this terminal illness and that you'd be dead in six months?" "That was his opinion," was the reply. The interviewer said, "Would you like to say more about that?" She said, "Well, you know we're told all these things by all these experts. We live on a farm, and all these federal people come in and they look at the soil and they tell us that nothing will grown and we should put these fertilizers in and we should do all this stuff. We don't do it and hell, things grow there anyway. So why would I listen to an expert?" I'm not saying to ignore your physician, but I'm saying that people of an independent mind and spirit seem to be people who have a better prognosis in these matters.

In summary I think that there is a lot we can learn by studying these kinds of things. We plan to gather people in remission; we hope to find out more about who they are, what they did and why they feel the way they feel.

Conclusion

I could go on with more and more of these stories, but time is limited. In conclusion let me mention some interesting clues coming now from the field of psychoneuroimmunology, that, as I said before, deals with the links between the brain, the mind and the immune system. We had thought that only those communications mediated in the mind/body system by the brain were important. But recently other systems have been discovered, and perhaps prematurely named -- though I think it's not premature myself — neuropeptide system. When I was doing brain research twenty years ago, injecting radioactive isotopes into rat brains and doing all kinds of horrible things that I've since stopped doing, we knew that there were substances in the brain that were responsible for the transmission of information in the brain. There were about three or four of them known in 1967. Today there are some fifty to sixty neuropeptides that are known, and what's very interesting is that they are being discovered all over the body. They're not just in the brain, they're in the gut, in the kidneys, throughout the system. This is a different system from the nervous system, though it is also part of the nervous system. Some of these same neuropeptides are found in cells of the immune system. So the whole picture of distinction between brain and body is getting much more blurred than it has been. I'll quote from an interesting book that I would recommend your reading. It's called *The Psychobiology of Mind/ Body Healing* by Ernest Rossi, just out from Norton Press. The last two paragraphs summarize where I think we may go with this in terms of the science of mind/body healing.

> Thus the slower-acting but more pervasive, flexible and unconscious func-
> tioning of the neuropeptide activity of mind/body communication more
> adequately fits the facts of hypnotic experience than the faster acting highly
> specific and consciously generated processes of the central and peripheral
> nervous systems. If we were to use a computer analogy, we could say that the
> peripheral nerves of the central nervous system are hardwired in a pre-set fixed
> pattern of stimulus and response, just as is the hardware of the computer. The
> neuropeptide system, however, is like the software of the computer that

contains the flexible, easily changed patterns of information. The receptors and highly individualized responses of the neuropeptide system are easily changed as a function of life experience, memory and learning. Neuropeptides, then, are a previously unrecognized form of information transduction between mind and body that may be the basis of many hypnotherapeutic, psychosocial and placebo responses.

From a broader perspective, the neuropeptide system may also be the psychobiological basis of the folk, shamanistic and spiritual forms of healing that share many of the characteristics of hypnotic healing and currently returning to vogue under the banner of wholistic medicine.

So there are some very interesting syntheses and fusions occurring. We at the Institute of Noetic Sciences are doing our best to spread seed grants around this country and maybe other countries to stimulate an integration of this kind of knowledge. We feel there is much to be learned from people in remission and people who have been healed in a spiritual way. They are, I think, our resource for the future.

Thank you.

MIRACLES STILL HAPPEN

By Robert Redd

The doctors came into the room where my son Jim and I were waiting anxiously. "Your wife has died," he said. "It must have been a lung embolism." I had a sudden stabbing feeling in my chest. The nurse rushed in, "We've got her going again." He quickly left for the operating room. That was the beginning of an episode which changed my life and presented experiences which are beyond belief.

The operation lasted nearly four hours. When the doctor returned he warned us, "There is less than a ten percent chance that she will survive the night." He explained the condition and all of the ramifications — peritonitis, toxic shock, DIC, adult respiratory syndrome — it went on.

That first night as I sat in the hospital, I thought: Where can I go? What should I do? I went into the chapel and I sat quietly for over an hour. While I was there a flower came into my mind's eye and this is the story of that flower.

In each of the four petals of the flower was a word. The first word was acceptance. How difficult it was for me to accept the possibility that my wife would die. How difficult it is to accept all the challenges and difficulties we face in our life today. Many times a person or experience can bring to us an unpleasant thought, an unpleasant feeling. We are constantly bombarded by fear, angry people, frustration. Many of the events that happen in our lives are not what we hoped for or planned. It's so hard to be accepting when we want things to come out the way we want them to be.

I'm reminded of Jesus as He faced that critical night in Gethsemane. He was faced with the possibility of fighting the Pharisees who were challenging his ideas. He could have escaped into the wilderness to wait for another time to come forth. But that would mean He didn't believe in what He was saying. So Jesus accepted what He had to accept. He faced the people and yielded in the face of the hostility. He let go and left it up to God.

History has shown that His life has had more effect on the world than any other man. The first petal of the flower was acceptance, and I continue to try to understand what acceptance means and to accept those things that I cannot change.

The second petal on the flower was patience. Those who know me would not describe me as patient. I'm known as Rapid Robert. Get it done now. I finished a four-year engineering degree in three years. Go-Go all the time. It's so human to want to see results and it's so difficult to trust that things will work out. Patience: waiting until the problem works its way through — believing that things will work out for the best — letting the process work itself through.

The third petal on the flower was relax. What a strange petal on a flower. At a time like this, how could I relax in the midst of all the turmoil, my wife possibly dying at the moment. Relax — and here came a key which I had no idea could be so powerful. In the years since that crisis, I've discovered that my ability to cope is determined by being able to relax — to let go of the stress. After my wife's illness, I became extremely stressed to the extent that I was threatened with severe hypertension. I went to the Mayo Clinic with blood pressure of 160/90. They did not give me medication; instead they taught me biofeedback — to relax.

Now three years later, my blood pressure is 110/60. I've learned that the biofeedback technique has a great deal of scientific support. When we are tense, the endocrine system generates chemicals such as adrenalin that cause us to want to fight or take flight. And these chemicals continually stimulate the body. They can cause heart disease, ulcers, and many other disease. The simple solution is to relax into the challenges that life brings us. Relax the hands and the arms and the chest, the shoulders, the eyes and the forehead and the jaw — and the whole body lets go. A miracle chemical in the body — called endorphin — provides a sense of well being. It can reduce pain, eliminate our anxiety, and lower our blood pressure. The miracle petal of relaxation, although it seemed so strange at that time, was an important key.

The fourth petal was love. Certainly my heart was surging with love. When I thought about my wife who for nearly 30 years had been my constant companion and support, I couldn't imagine living without her. I thought about our 30th anniversary we were planning in September, only two months away. I thought about the sixth grandchild we were expecting.

I thought about the vacation we were planning in the fall. All of this was in my heart. I realized without love, life has no meaning. So much of our life is pursuing money and power. Now it all seemed so useless. Now my only concern was my loving wife. Probably no one could ever say it any better than St. Paul did in *Corinthians*, but if you have lost a loved one you understand love is the essence of life.

So there was my flower — acceptance, patience, relax, and love. But there was more. There was a stem of the flower and on the stem was written "Trust in God." And so I did.

That was the beginning of a long siege of hospital stays; night and day attendance with my wife. My sons came to join us in our vigil. For over forty-five days, we stood by her bedside, encouraged her, and prayed for her. We secured enormous support from many churches, Ann's friends, and our loved ones. The nurses and doctors were magnificent. For some reason, which is yet to be discovered, she survived the entire ordeal and became healthy again. "A miracle," the doctor said when he discharged her from the hospital. "There is no question, this is a miracle." Very, very few people have ever survived any one of these afflictions at the age of 58 and she survived them all.

I share this story with you to affirm that miracles are possible. That simple flower continues to challenge me today. I intend to spend the rest of my life trying to live the message of the vision. The petals arranged in a simple pattern of four, opposite each other, spinning into infinity — acceptance, patience, relaxation, and love. From this stem it reaches deep into the heart of our unconscious; the energy flows into our lives — Trust in God.

Choices, For Your Third Age, December, 1987.

Once you have accepted His plan
as the one function that you would fulfill,
there will be nothing else
the Holy Spirit will not arrange for you
without your effort.
He will go before you
making straight your path,
and leaving in your way no stones
to trip on, and no obstacles
to bar your way.
Nothing you need will be denied you.
Not one seeming difficulty
but will melt away before you reach it.
You need take thought for nothing,
careless of everything
except the only purpose
that you would fulfill.

A Course In Miracles   *Text*   *Page 404*

REFERENCES

Achterberg, Jeanne. *Imagery in Healing*. New Science Library, Boston and London, 1985.

California Task Force to Promote Self-Esteem and Personal and Social Responsibility; Toward a State of Esteem. California State Department of Education, 1990.

Callari, Elizabeth. *A Gentle Death*. MacMillan Publishing Company, New York, NY, 1985.

Coit, Lee. *Listening*. Swan Publishers, S. Laguna, CA. 1985.

Crandall, Joanne. *Self-Transformation Through Music*. The Theosophical Publishing House, Wheaton, IL, 1986.

Dass, Ram and Gorman, Paul. *How Can I Help?* Alfred A. Knopf, New York, NY, 1985.

Dass, Ram. *Journey of Awakening*. Bantam Books, New York, NY, 1978.

Duba, Deborah. *Coming Home: A Guide to Dying at Home with Dignity*. Aurora Press, Inc., New York, NY, 1987.

Edwards, Betty. *Drawing on the Right Side of the Brain*. Jeremy P. Tarcher, Inc., Los Angeles, CA, 1979.

Hay, Louise L. *You Can Heal Your Life*. Hay House, 3029 Wilshire Blvd., Santa Monica, CA 90404.

Foundation for Inner Peace, *A Course In Miracles*. Coleman Graphics, Huntington Station, NY, 1975.

Foundation for Inner Peace, *A Song of Prayer*. Coleman Graphics, Huntington Station, NY, 1975.

Jampolsky, Gerald, M.D. *Love is Letting Go of Fear*. Celestial Arts, Millbrae, CA, 1979.

Jampolsky, Gerald, M.D. *Good-Bye to Guilt*. Bantam Books, New York, NY, 1985.

Jampolsky, Gerald, M.D. *Teach Only Love*. Bantam Books, New York, NY, 1983.

Kubler-Ross, Elisabeth. *On Children and Death*. MacMillan Publishing Company, New York, NY, 1985.

Lusseryan, Jacques. "Jeremy". *PARABOLA, The Magazine of Myth and Tradition*, Volume XI, Number 2, May, 1986.

Eastern News, Sandusky, OH.

Mathews-Simonton, Stephanie, Simonton, O. Carl, M.D. and Creighton, James L. *Getting Well Again*. Bantam Books, New York, NY, 1985.

O'Regan, Brendan. "Healing, Remission and Miracle Cures". Institute of Noetic Sciences publication, Sausalito, CA. 94966-0097, Summer, 1987.

Paramananda, Swami. *Christ and Oriental Ideals*. Vedanta Center, Inc., Cohasset, MA, 1968.

Ravindra, Ravi. "The Gospel as Yoga". *Parabola*, Summer, 1988, Volume XIII, Number 2, May, 1968.

Redd, Robert. "Miracles Still Happen". *Choices For Your Third Age*, Grand Rapids, MI, December, 1987.

Schoenhals, Karen. "If You Should Meet a Dying Child", *Evangelizing Today's Child*, Volume 8, N6, 1981.

Seigel, Bernard, M.D. *Love, Medicine and Miracles*. Harper and Row, New York, NY, 1986.

Stauffer, Edith R., Ph.D. *Unconditional Love and Forgiveness*. Triangle Publishers, Burbank, CA 91507, 1987.

Syed, Dr. M. MA, Ph.D. *Thus Spake Prophet Muhammad*. Sri Ramakrishna Math, Madras 60004, India, 1977.

The Children at the Center for Attitudinal Healing, Tiburon, CA. *Another Look at the Rainbow*. Celestial Arts, Milbrae, CA, 1982.

The Children at the Center for Attitudinal Healing, Tiburon, CA. *There is a Rainbow Behind Every Dark Cloud*. Celestial Arts, Milbrae, CA, 1978.

ATTITUDINAL HEALING CENTER REFERENCE LIST

ALABAMA

Alabama Center for Attitudinal Healing
c/o Unity
2803 Highland Avenue South
Birmingham, Alabama 35205

ARIZONA

Wholeness Center
3205 North 70th Street
Scottsdale, Arizona 85711
Anya Woody
602-946-2114, 602-937-2389

Center for Life Awareness
11001 North 24th Avenue #612
Phoenix, Arizona 85029

CALIFORNIA

Center for Attitudinal Healing
19 Main Street
Tiburon, California 94920
415-435-5022

East Bay Center
7 Van Sicklen Place
Oakland, California 94610
Janice McNeal
415-893-5683

Eureka
1088 Port Kenyon Road
Ferndale, California 95536
Pat and Dane Cowan
707-786-9904 (home)
707-443-2722 (office)
707-735-5268 (office)

Mendocino/Ukiah
Life-Threatened Group
Michael Murphy
707-462-1553

Morgan Hill Center
2320 Shafer Avenue
Morgan Hill, California 95037
Gail Byrum
408-778-3346

West Oakland Center for Attitudinal Healing
Post Office Box 23503
Oakland, California 94610
Aeeshah Ababio
415-536-4600

Santa Cruz Center for Attitudinal Healing
2803 Branciforte Drive
Santa Cruz, California 95065
408-427-2798

Sonoma Center for Attitudinal Healing
3925 Sumner Lane
Santa Rosa, California 95405
Linda Abrahams
707-586-9381

San Fernando Valley, California
Angie Pike
818-885-7288
Rue Baron
818-349-1261

Orange County, California
Dan Millstein
714-556-8000
Gina Russell
714-968-0540

COLORADO

Attitudinal Healing Center
1006 Robertson #A
Ft. Collins, Colorado 80524-3925
Gwyn Cody
303-482-4156

CONNECTICUT
ECap (Exceptional Cancer Patients)
1302 Chapel Street
New Haven, Connecticut 06511
Bernie Siegel
203-865-8392

DISTRICT OF COLOMBIA

Institute for Attitudinal Studies
4530 - 16th Street NW
mail: Post Office Box 40901
Washington, D. C. 20016
Susan Trout
202-726-6200

FLORIDA

Aslan House, Attitudinal Healing Center
Post Office Box 52116
Jacksonville, Florida 32201
Paula Hinson
904-353-4357

Miami Center for Attitudinal Healing
8345 Carol Way
Miami, Florida 33155
Bill Brunelle
305-271-5121

Project Rainbow/Family Services
9009 Seminole Blvd. #28
Seminole, Florida 34642
813-397-7200

The Life Center
214 South Fielding Avenue
Tampa, Florida 33606
Sheryle Baker
813-251-0289

GEORGIA

Center for Attitudinal Awareness
Post Office Box 675015
Marietta, Georgia 30067
Pat Zerman
404-953-3136

HAWAII

The Maui Center for Attitudinal Healing
Post Office Box 134
Kahului, Hawaii 96732
Carol William
808-242-6187

Kauai Attitudinal Healing Center
3420 B Kuhio Highway
Lihue, Hawaii 96766
Linda and Neil Sutherland, M.D.
808-245-1553

ILLINOIS

Chicago Center for Attitudinal Change
410 West Grant Place
Chicago, Illinois 60614
Carolyn Schuham
312-871-0866

INDIANA

Indianapolis Center for Attitudinal Healing
3402 Boulevard Place
Indianapolis, Indiana 46208
Gerry Rhea
317-924-2324

IOWA

Quad Cities Child and Family Support
718 Bridge Avenue, Suite 6
Davenport, Iowa 52803
Darla Lemke
319-324-2617

KANSAS

Myrtle Filmore Center
3834 West 75th Street
Prairie Village, Kansas 66208
913-722-2900
913-776-1465

KENTUCKY

Life Center for Attitudinal Healing
11803 Old Shelbyville Road, #5
Middletown, Kentucky 40243-1476

LOUISIANA

Peace Center for Attitudinal Healing
744 Slattery Blvd.
Shreveport, Louisana 71104
Terry Coutret
318-865-4705

MARYLAND

Baltimore Center for Attitudinal Healing
Post Office Box 65125
Baltimore, Maryland 21209
301-882-0398

MASSACHUSETTS

Sherborn Center
2 North Main Street
Sherborn, Massachusetts 01770
Louis Randa
508-650-3659

MICHIGAN

Grand Rapids Center for Attitudinal Healing
48 South Division Street
Grand Rapids, Michigan 49503
Ginny Weirich
616-459-2204

Attitudinal Health Program
The Fetzer Institute
9292 West KL Avenue
Kalamazoo, Michigan 49009
Carolyn Dailey
616-375-2000

MINNESOTA

The Minnesota Center for Attitudinal Healing
22020 Juniper Street NW
Cedar, Minnesota 55011
Luann Poulson
612-753-2490

MISSOURI

St. Louis Center for Attitudinal Healing
Post Office Box 12845
St. Louis, Missouri 63141
Nancy Jeffers
314-230-0800

MONTANA

Big Sky Center for Attitudinal Healing
201 University Avenue
Missoula, Montana 59801
Sigrun Johnson
406-728-2084

NEW MEXICO
Attitudinal Healing Center
Post Office Box 40162
Albuquerque, New Mexico 87196
505-256-7010

Life Center for Attitudinal Healing
1418 Luisa Street, #4
mail: Post Office Box 8718
Santa Fe, New Mexico 87504
505-983-5541

OHIO

Cincinnati Center for Attitudinal Healing
Post Office Box 42204
Cincinnati, Ohio 45242
Karen Warren
513-753-7006

Rainbow Center for Attitudinal Healing
Post Office Box 2802
Toledo, Ohio 43606
Carol Stacy
419-478-0202

PENNSYLVANIA

Foundation for Well Being
(Attitudinal Healing Center of the Delaware
  Valley)
46 Red Rowan Lane
Plymouth Meeting, Pennsylvania 19462
Philip Friedman
215-828-4674

TEXAS

Austin Center for Attitudinal Healing
1032 Capital Parkway
Austin, Texas 78746
512-327-1961

Attitudinal Healing Center 1017 S. Staples
Corpus Christi, Texas 78404
Rusty Barrier
512-882-4820

The Houston Center for Attitudinal Healing
Post Office Box 541972
Houston, Texas 77254-1972
713-789-7682

Katy Life Center
20523 Manette Drive
Katy, Texas 77450
Carolyn Brenner
713-492-2218

Dallas Center for Attitudinal Healing
4054 McKinney #201
Dallas, Texas 75205
Judy Arkow
214-301-6217

WASHINGTON

Northwest Center for Attitudinal Healing
11700 First Avenue NE
Seattle, Washington 98125
206-362-3897

WISCONSIN

The Wellness Counseling Center
100 West Lawrence Street
Appleton, Wisconsin 54911
414-733-1992

AUSTRALIA

John Swinburne
Post Office Box 54
Cleveland, Queensland 4163

The Melbourne Living Centre
216 Mahoneys Road
Burwood East, Victoria 3151
David McCrae
03-887-9866

Patricia and Don Michalka
14 Lichendale Street
Floreat Park, 6014 Perth
011-619-387-5568 (home)
011-619-387-8855 (office)

Very Special Kids
31 Alma Road
St. Kilda, Victoria 3101
Sr. Margaret Noone
03-525-3383

Living Centre
360 Mt. Albert Road
Mont Albert, Victoria 3127
03-890-2209

Townsville Centre for Attitudinal Healing
26 Marron Crescent
Mundingberra, Queensland

Jill Gardner
64a Darling Street
Balmain, New South Wales 2041

Shirley Lewis
23 Armstrong Street
Wentworth Falls, New South Wales 2782
047-572185

CANADA

Rainbow Centre
785 Cactus Road
Kelowna, British Columbia VIX 3N5
Norma Selbie
604-860-7414

The L.I.F.E. Project
(Vancouver Island Centre for Attitudinal
    Healing)
#1 - 2520 Bowen Road
Nanaimo, British Columbia V9T 3L3
Roberta Scotthorne
604-756-1652

Winnepeg Centre for Attitudinal Healing
Post Office Box 1
St. Norbert, Manitoba R3V 1L5
Gwen Peters
204-269-1502

Le Fil d'Or (The Golden Thread)
Quebec
Lise Brousseau
514-598-8096
Sylvia Larouche
514-523-8830

ARGENTINA

El Centro Actitudes que Sanan
Las Heras 2062 - 1 Piso
1127 Buenos Aires
Alberto Loizaga
803-6865
803-6115

CHILE

Aguaviva
Santa Blanca 1756 La De Hesa
Santiago, Chile
Jimena de Mortimer
215-1506

GREAT BRITAIN

Centre for Attitudinal Healing/London
Post Office Box 2023
London W12 9NY, England

Bristol Centre for Attitudinal Healing
33 Colston Fort, Montague Place
Kingsdown, Bristol BS6 5UB
Lynne Watterson

Pauline Crump
Marion Cottage, Stokenham
Nr. Kingsbridge, Devon, TQ7 2S2

BELGIUM

Attitudinal Healing Centre
Sellaerstraat 40
1820 Melsbroek, Belgium
02-751-72-43

GERMANY

Rainbow Center
Ammerseestrasse 18
8208 Kolbermoor, West Germany
Karen Fursich
08031-94804

HOLLAND

Willem Glaudemans
Treek 22
3524 TA Utrecht
030-895613

MEXICO

Maria Cde Candano
Bosque del Molino 16
La Herradura, Mexico 10, D. F.
525-589-8908

NEW ZEALAND

Auckland Center for Attitudinal Healing
Post Office Box 2063
Auckland John and Cathy Carter

Margaret Johnstone
51 Te Awa Avenue
Napier, Hawke Bay

Jean and Allan Batham
Rural Delivery 1, Onerahi
Whangarei
089-437-5711

SWITZERLAND

Karin Wachsmuth
43 Rt de Prevessin
CH 1217
Meyrin, Switzerland
22 7824790